GLOBAL COMPANIES & PUBLIC POLICY

GLOBAL COMPANIES & PUBLIC POLICY

THE GROWING CHALLENGE OF FOREIGN DIRECT INVESTMENT

DeAnne Julius

PUBLISHED IN NORTH AMERICA FOR

THE ROYAL INSTITUTE OF INTERNATIONAL AFFAIRS

COUNCIL ON FOREIGN RELATIONS PRESS
• NEW YORK •

Chatham House Papers

General Series Editor: William Wallace
International Economics Programme Director: J.M.C. Rollo

The Royal Institute of International Affairs, at Chatham House in London, has provided an impartial forum for discussion and debate on current international issues for 70 years. Its resident research fellows, specialized information resources, and range of publications, conferences, and meetings span the fields of international politics, economics, and security. The Institute is independent of government.

Chatham House Papers are short monographs on current policy problems which have been commissioned by the RIIA. In preparing the papers, authors are advised by a study group of experts convened by the RIIA, and publication of a paper indicates that the Institute regards it as an authoritative contribution to the public debate. The Institute does not, however, hold opinions of its own; the views expressed in this publication are the responsibility of the author.

Library of Congress Cataloguing-in-Publication Data

Julius, DeAnne S., 1949–.
 Global companies and public policy : the growing challenge of foreign investment / by DeAnne Julius.
  p.   cm.—(Chatham House papers)
 ISBN 0-87609-083-8 : $14.95
 1. International business enterprises.   2. Investments, Foreign.
3. International economic relations.   I. Royal Institute of
International Affairs.   II. Title.   III. Series: Chatham House
papers (Unnumbered)
HD2755.5.J85   1990
332.6'73—dc20   90-1643
                                                       CIP

90 91 92 93 94 95 96 PB 10 9 8 7 6 5 4 3 2 1

CONTENTS

Contents

TABLES AND FIGURES

Tables

Figures

For Megan and Ross

PREFACE

The interest of research fellows at the Royal Institute of International Affairs in the subject of foreign direct investment has a pedigree stretching back at least to 1937. That was the year in which a study group chaired by H.D. Henderson and including J.M. Keynes produced a 360-page book on *The Problem of International Investment*. The 'problem' to which they referred was the failure of investment flows to revive sufficiently after World War I to effect the rebuilding of Europe, in the same way that pre-war investment from Europe had accelerated the development of the Americas. Without flows from abroad to relieve capital and foreign exchange constraints, protectionism grew, trade shrank, major countries slid into depression and, eventually, into World War II.

How the problem of international investment has changed! By the 1960s American investment in Europe was so large that it aroused widespread fear and resentment of *le défi américain* (Servan-Schreiber, 1968). A 1971 study on *The Multinationals* by the current Chairman of the Royal Institute of International Affairs, Christopher Tugendhat, drew attention to the growing influence of multinational business on international trade and finance, and predicted that tensions between governments and international companies would grow. Sure enough, by 1984 a Chatham House Paper was needed on *Inward Investment: Policy Options for the United Kingdom* (Brech and Sharp, 1984). The recent emergence of the Japanese as international investors sharpened this concern. Louis Turner's 1987 Chatham House Paper on *Industrial Collaboration with Japan* analyses the nature and impact of Japanese activity on European business.

Meanwhile, for the first time, inward investment has become a contentious issue in the United States. Following on from Louis Turner's work, Stephen Thomsen and I began to assemble the data for a comparative cross-country study of both inward and outward direct investment. What we felt was missing from the current debate was the global perspective (evident in the 1937 study) of foreign direct investment as a macroeconomic phenomenon, linking home and foreign markets, and creating the same dynamic of positive-sum growth as gains from trade. The analogy with trade also has important implications for policy towards foreign investment by both home and host countries.

As the recent growth and current size of these flows became apparent from our research, this perspective led me to question the way in which economists conventionally view external imbalances between countries and the exchange-rate prescriptions to which such views give rise. Such questions lay outside the scope of our original research, but they are fundamental to understanding how modern economies are linked and, thus, what sort of international policy framework (post-GATT or ultra-GATT) will be needed in a world in which global companies access more foreign markets through direct investment than through trade. I have tried to raise these larger questions in a systematic way and have attempted an initial approach (in Chapter 4) for addressing them. I hope that this will stimulate the further research that will be necessary to substantiate (or not) the ideas put forward.

In addition to drawing inspiration from past work at Chatham House and elsewhere, I benefited greatly from the input of the members of a study group which met at Chatham House during 1989. My deepest thanks to all members of the group, and especially to its chairman, William Wallace, both for his constant challenge to look 'beyond economics' and for his unfailing support, even while labouring under his own writing deadlines. Steve Thomsen's role as collaborative researcher was essential to the success of the project, and his own writing in this field has made an important contribution to my thinking. I am grateful to Phedon Nicolaides for taking on many of my responsibilities at Chatham House during the final writing phase, and to Peter Kenen for his germane advice, both while he was a visiting fellow and later through his comments on the manuscript. My unflappable and efficient secretary, Kathy Oswald, held the whole show together and expertly steered the manuscript through its successive drafts. Finally, I am grateful to Pauline Wickham and her staff for their smooth and timely management of the publication process.

Funding for the project was provided by the Corporate Sponsors of the RIIA International Economics Programme and by the Tokyo Club Foundation for Global Studies. In earlier stages of the research I benefited greatly from the comments and suggestions of my Tokyo Club colleagues from the Nomura Research Institute, the Brookings Institution, the IFO Institute and IFRI.

The paper was written while I was Director of Economics at Chatham House. The views expressed in it, and any remaining mistakes, are my own and should not be attributed to the RIIA or the project sponsors.

January 1990   DeAnne Julius

GLOBAL COMPANIES & PUBLIC POLICY

1

INTRODUCTION

The 1980s have been a perplexing decade for economic forecasters and policy analysts. The most respected international think-tanks, as well as the establishment forecasters at the IMF and the OECD, have seen their projections fall embarrassingly short of reality, and heard their warnings echo hollowly as the dire consequences failed to materialize. For more than five years we have been worrying about the triggering of a 'dollar freefall' or 'hard landing' that could provoke a recession in the United States and beyond (Marris, 1985). During this time the dollar has indeed fallen – by over 40% in trade-weighted terms – but economic growth in the US and the rest of the OECD actually accelerated. The stock market crash that rippled round the world in October 1987 caused the OECD and nearly all lesser economic forecasters to lower their growth projections and to support a concerted monetary expansion by the major central banks. With hindsight, that expansion was probably unnecessary; the real economy chugged merrily ahead, seemingly oblivious of the shock in its financial counterpart.

The most bewildering gap between the accepted wisdom of policy analysts and the actual economic developments of the 1980s concerns the importance and impact of the large trade imbalances that have emerged among the major countries. Worries about the US deficit and the Japanese and German surpluses have dominated the international economic policy debate. Economists and policy-makers from Europe, the US and Japan have shown a remarkable degree of agreement that the budget and current account 'twin deficits' of the United States are a grave threat to world economic growth. The accounting identity links between the export-import gap and the savings-investment gap have been trotted out again and again to urge tax increases and dollar depreciation on the US and fiscal stimulus in Japan and Germany. Yet without major action on any of these fronts since 1986, the OECD economies continued to outperform nearly all forecasts.

Is apocalypse around the corner, or must we begin to question the continued relevance of mainstream international economic theory as a tool for policy analysis? Are we misinterpreting the linkages between the real and the financial markets at the international level? Are the channels of policy influence more diffuse than we realize? More generally, have supply-side developments in modern economies undermined our basic understanding of what drives growth and what triggers recession? Is there a new growth dynamic at work that we are failing to perceive? And, if so, what does this imply for the international economy of the 1990s and for the role and jurisdiction of economic policy-makers?

This paper does not attempt to provide conclusive answers to such questions. Rather, it is focused on one important development in the 1980s: the remarkable creation and expansion of global companies. However, when this phenomenon was examined, using evidence from five major countries, it became apparent that there have been significant changes in the character and strength of the linkages between national economies.* The broad questions raised in this introductory chapter provide a perspective for what follows, but they emerged at the end, rather than the beginning, of our work, as we began to appreciate the macroeconomic implications of the findings and came to believe that the analytical models which currently shape economic policy prescriptions have been sadly inadequate for the 1980s and may be dangerously misleading for the 1990s.

The organizing principle for the research was to use a multi-country, multi-directional framework to analyse flows of foreign direct investment (FDI), to relate these flows to national economy aggregates (such as output, employment, or investment) and to trace the implications for linkages across economies of the growing stocks of foreign-held assets. Too often the public debate focuses on one-way, single-country, analyses. This leads to fears that foreigners are

*The original work on foreign direct investment on which our research has been based was funded partly by the *Tokyo Club Foundation for Global Studies* and early results were published in the *Tokyo Club Papers* (1988, 1989). The project was carried out at the Royal Institute of International Affairs by DeAnne Julius and Stephen Thomsen.

'buying up the country' or that domestic industry is 'exporting jobs' by investing overseas. By looking at both inward and outward direct investment and by using a five-country sample, one can develop comparative insights and an overview on the size and importance of these flows for the world economy in the years to come.

This chapter describes the historical and macroeconomic context against which the FDI flows of the 1980s are set. For those readers unfamiliar with the traditional economic paradigms that come in for criticism later, it also provides a thumbnail sketch of the basic models of international trade and finance, including exchange-rate behaviour.

Chapters 2 and 3 present the comparative figures on inward and outward FDI flows by the Group of Five (G-5) countries over the last decade. Outward FDI is considered in Chapter 2. It looks particularly at the oldest and largest investors – the United States and Britain – and relates their experience to the development of Japan as an emerging major player. To explore the implications for the future, a scenario of outward FDI flows to the year 1995 is built up from assumptions based on the comparative analysis across countries and recent historical trends.

Inward investment flows for the G-5 are examined in Chapter 3 and the evidence for and argument over the costs and benefits of such flows are summarized. The scenario analysis is completed by projecting the distribution of inward flows and deriving a matrix of inward/outward investment for the US, the European Community, Japan and the rest of the world in 1995. This shows that even under conservative assumptions, the global stock of FDI by 1995 will be more than double (2.2 times) the 1988 stock in real terms. There is a near doubling of current annual flows, which themselves have exploded since 1983. The European Community sees the largest increase in inward investment, but sizeable inflows continue in the US and, for the first time, Japan is exposed to significant inward investment.

Chapter 4 looks at the central linkage between investment and trade flows. It shows that for the US and Japan, FDI-related trade – i.e., trade between foreign-owned firms and their home countries – already accounts for half of total trade flows. It proposes a new paradigm for considering a country's total foreign sales and purchases, including those made in overseas markets by the foreign subsidiaries of its own firms, rather than just its exports and imports, as an alternative indicator of its international competitiveness. When such 'ownership-based trade measures' are calculated for the US and Japan, they contrast dramatically with the picture of current account imbalances. On an ownership basis, the greater integration of the US economy with the rest of the world, compared to Japan, is revealed and its net trade deficit becomes a net surplus of ownership-based foreign sales over foreign purchases. The implications of this approach for exchange rates are explored.

Finally, Chapter 5 explores the policy implications of this process of FDI-led economic integration among the advanced countries. It proposes a new framework for inward investment policy and considers the impact of FDI-led integration on economic growth in the 1990s and on the stability of the world economy.

The historical and economic context

Chapters 2 and 3 document the tidal wave of cross-border investment by private companies that this decade has witnessed. These flows are growing much faster than world trade, a large portion of which is pulled along in their wake. In the advanced economies of the OECD, foreign-owned firms now account for a significant share of 'domestic' output, employment and investment, as well as trade.

In some ways we are witnessing the continuation of an interrupted trend that began in the 1960s with the rapid growth of American investment in Europe. Although international companies existed long before then, it was argued convincingly in 1971 that 'the 1960s was a new era' in the growth of international companies (Tugendhat, 1971; Vernon, 1977). Prior to that decade, most multinational enterprises (MNEs) had the bulk of their foreign investment in the developing countries, and the dominant organizational pattern was for each affiliate to be as self-contained as possible – small clones, scattered round the world, of the mother company. Developments in transport and communications technology permitted the emergence in the 1960s of a more centralized organizational structure, where production and financing decisions were taken at headquarters and allocated across subsidiaries. Tugendhat shows how this centralized pattern of control enabled companies to reap efficiency gains in raising capital (especially on the Eurodollar markets) and in 'evening out the trade cycle' by shifting production from plants in countries of high domestic demand to those operating below capacity due to slack demand – thereby raising the exports of the slack economy and increasing the imports of the booming economy. By the 1980s, this process seems to have contributed to a situation where differential growth/recession patterns among the major economies have themselves been evened out, and the entire OECD moves through cycles together.

Like so many other economic trends, the advance of MNEs was halted during the 1970s by the economic problems that resulted from the oil and other commodity price shocks beginning in 1973. Policy-makers groped for ways to smooth the massive recycling of funds that these generated, and to manage the slowdown in their own oil-importing economies. Recession at home and heightened uncertainty abroad made the MNEs cautious. Then the coordinated economic stimulus applied by the Group of Seven (G-7) countries in the mid-1970s – the 'locomotive' theory – proved too much and, coupled with another oil price shock in 1979, sent inflation into double digits.

The new chairman of the US Federal Reserve Board, Paul Volcker, and the new British Prime Minister, Margaret Thatcher, independently but simultaneously adopted monetarism as their guiding principle for monetary policy. Tightening the growth of their respective money supplies sent interest rates to record levels, provoking a major recession in nearly all OECD countries by the early 1980s.

It is thus apparent with hindsight that this roller-coaster of economic behaviour was destabilized by badly timed or excessive policy responses to large external shocks. At the time, all the private sector could do was to act defensively. Many of the non-oil American MNEs actually reduced their overseas exposure by heavy profit repatriation. The trough of US foreign direct investment flows was reached in 1983.

Two lessons stand out from this experience of the 1970s. First, coordinated policy by the G-7 can have very powerful effects, but the lag between policy implementation and the economy's response is sometimes a long one. This implies that coordinated policies should be applied gradually and cautiously. Too much hype – about either the problems or the solutions – can raise public expectations that make it more difficult for political leaders to await the results of past actions and resist turning up the controls another notch. Second, however, if extremes of inflation or unemployment are reached, behavioural patterns take over in the private sector which make the reversal of those extremes very difficult to set in train. This was understood simultaneously by Paul Volcker in the US and by Margaret Thatcher in the UK. Both, in their own quite separate ways, accompanied the shock treatments they administered to their respective economies in 1979–82 with uncompromising announcements of new policies that were designed as much to reverse public expectations as to affect the economic aggregates. In effect, the policy-maker is steering the economy along a reasonably wide track, with steep drop-offs on either side and a loose linkage between the steering controls and the wheels.

Since the early 1980s the OECD economies – and their drivers – have been performing rather well. Confidence has returned in the private sector and the growth both of world trade and of cross-border investment has resumed apace. Compared to the pattern of the 1960s, the latter has exploded. Whereas in the 1960s FDI grew at twice the rate of GNP, in the 1980s it has grown more than four times as fast as GNP. In the 1960s, American companies accounted for nearly two-thirds of cross-border investment; in the 1980s British and Japanese FDI has grown much faster than that of the US and a more even distribution of foreign ownership across countries is now emerging. In addition, the fastest growth of FDI in the 1980s has been in the service sectors, not in traditional manufacturing as in the 1960s. It is no longer just the largest companies that have gone global; a growing proportion of FDI is from medium-size and even small companies.

Thus the 1980s have brought more than a resumption of the cross-border investment trends of the 1960s. Not only has FDI in the 1980s grown even faster than it did in the 1960s, but it is changing in character. We have moved beyond the one-dimensional flows of the 1960s that provoked Europeans to worry about *le défi américain* (Servan-Schreiber, 1968). We are rapidly approaching a new level of economic integration through direct investment: a cascading of flows from more countries, into more sectors and involving more actors than ever before. Unlike trade, these FDI flows represent long-term commitments by companies to build viable businesses in one another's markets. They may be slowed, but they will not easily be reversed, by economic downturns or shifts in exchange rates. It is time to examine what effects such long-term linkages among economies are likely to have both on the stability and management of the world economy and on the already weakening political support in the major democracies for an open trade and investment regime.

The analytical tools

As a specialization within economics, international trade and finance has a long and distinguished history, and it has produced a recent crop of new shoots such as 'strategic trade policy' and 'international macro'. These are reviewed briefly in Chapter 3, where it is argued that the development of more sophisticated tools has not yielded a commensurate gain in understanding how economies interact, although it has produced some specific insights applicable to very particular circumstances. It has also been shown that one of the major weaknesses of – and sources of disagreement among – econometric models which attempt to cover more than one country is the way they portray exchange rate behaviour and the international adjustment process (Isard, 1988). In this sense, the development of more sophisticated tools has only served to show us more clearly what we do *not* understand.

If recent theoretical contributions shed little light, it is necessary to return to first principles. Are any of the critical underpinnings of our basic international economic theories seriously weakened by the changes that the world economy has undergone since they were developed? This question is explored in the empirical chapters that follow. For the non-economist reader, the two relevant branches of this basic body of theory to which future chapters refer – international trade and international finance – are briefly surveyed here.

International trade theory

The modern theory of international trade, like so many other aspects of modern economics, traces its beginnings to Adam Smith. It was in *The Wealth of Nations* (1776) that he identified the fundamental fallacy of the mercantilists and showed how trade between countries brings benefits to both because it enables both to consume more (without the need for one to have a surplus or the other a deficit). Forty years later another British economist, David Ricardo, developed an important extension of Smith's insight by showing that trade between countries would be to their mutual benefit even if one of the countries had an *absolute* advantage in the

7

production of all the traded products (that is, even if it were the lowest cost producer of all). Only the weak postulate of *comparative* advantage is required for trade to be mutually beneficial. Comparative advantage exists whenever the *relative* costs of products are different in the two countries. In Ricardo's theory the difference in costs is due to differences in the productivity of labour per unit of output in each industry in the two countries.

In the 1920s two Swedish economists, Eli Heckscher and Bertil Ohlin, developed what has become the conventional explanation of the source of comparative advantage; namely, the factor endowment of countries. The basic idea is that a country with an abundant supply of labour can produce labour-intensive goods relatively cheaply and therefore it will specialize in – and export – those goods while importing capital-intensive goods, produced by countries with abundant supplies of capital. This clearly assumes that the factors of production (i.e., labour, capital, land, entrepreneurship) do not themselves cross boundaries, although some of them may change over time within countries thereby modifying the country's comparative advantage (the Rybczynski theorem, developed by a contemporary British economist in 1955). This basic model of comparative advantage based on factor endowments has been greatly extended and refined since the 1920s – notably by Samuelson in the 1940s, and many others since – but it remains the cornerstone of international trade theory. While modern trade theorists employ a much richer and more complex set of theories of trade, the Heckscher-Ohlin version still underpins the approach of most economists and enlightened policy-makers when confronting trade policy issues.

In recent years an offshoot sometimes known as the 'strategic trade' literature has developed. It focuses on industries and markets where economies of scale or other imperfectly competitive features create natural barriers to entry for potential newcomers. This work has shed new light on the basis for trade in differentiated products and thus for intra-industry trade. However, its trade policy prescriptions, based on strategic interactions, are more controversial. Most economists accept the mathematical result that under certain imperfectly competitive conditions trade barriers will yield higher national gains than free trade. However, the conditions for deriving such conclusions are thought to apply to very few industries in the modern world. In addition, the information needs for calculating appropriate tariffs are extensive, and politically motivated retaliation by trade partners is probable. Thus, paradoxically, the strategic literature can be interpreted as strengthening the bias in favour of open trade policies by showing how restrictive the requirements are to justify exceptions (Krugman, 1987).

International finance theory

The other branch of economic thought that is particularly relevant to international policy questions is the international finance literature on exchange rate regimes. Again 'modern' economic thought began with the discrediting of the mercantilists – this time by Scottish economist David Hume who showed in 1752 that under the gold standard a permanent payments surplus was impossible, and thus made no sense as a policy objective. Similarly, a payments deficit would set in train forces which would reduce it, and thus a country did not have to worry about losing all its gold. Hume elaborated the automatic adjustment process of the gold standard (the 'price-specie-flow' mechanism) by which prices would be bid up in countries with gold inflows resulting from trade surpluses, thereby reducing the competitiveness of their exports and eventually decreasing their surpluses.

The policy implication of Hume's world of flexible domestic price levels and fixed exchange rates anchored to gold is that governments need not concern themselves with external imbalances because they will be self-correcting over time. Once the world moved off the gold standard, governments gained both an additional policy instrument (their exchange rate) and an additional target (external balance). Much of the economic literature in this field from the 1930s to the end of the 1960s concerned the differing routes by which a currency devaluation could correct a payments deficit, and the conditions under which that might fail to happen. The 'absorption approach', developed by Sidney Alexander (1952), showed that devaluation can improve the trade balance only if it increases real income or cuts real expenditure. This is unlikely to happen unless the economy has idle resources at the beginning. Others developed the 'elasticities approach' to explain what happens when prices change but incomes are held constant (Robinson, 1937). Finally, the Nobel-prize-winning British economist, James Meade, brought these strands together in his 'synthesis theory' which set out the conditions that had to be met for a country to achieve both internal and external balance (Meade, 1951). His basic conclusion was that a country

9

needed one set of policies to influence the level of domestic demand (typically fiscal and monetary policies) and another set to influence the composition of demand between domestic and imported goods. In this latter category of policies, he included exchange rate changes, tariffs, export subsidies and other types of protection.

Meanwhile, at the IMF the Dutch economist J.J. Polak brought attention back to the role of money and domestic price adjustments in achieving external balance through depreciation. In what came to be known as the 'monetary approach' to the balance of payments – also elaborated at the University of Chicago by Canadian economists Robert Mundell and Harry Johnson – the role of domestic credit creation (the money supply) in prolonging external imbalances or preventing their correction is explored (Polak, 1957). External payments deficits can only persist as long as domestic credit creation is excessive. Thus a devaluation will be most successful in correcting an external deficit if it is accompanied by a domestic credit squeeze. This prescription has become uncomfortably familiar to those countries – including Britain – which have come under IMF tutelage; it has also proved its robustness over a wide variety of circumstances.

Most of this work related to a world of fixed exchange rates which were occasionally adjusted by governments. Another set of theories has been developed to deal with a world of floating exchange rates, whose values are set by markets. The main question asked by this work is what relationship exists between variables which are still under the control of governments – such as domestic interest rates and the budget deficit – and the market-determined exchange rate. By using its monetary and fiscal policy tools, how can a government achieve its desired levels of income and inflation with floating exchange rates and – most theories add – free capital movements?

The Mundell-Fleming model developed in the early 1960s has become the classic framework used to explore such questions. Its major innovation is the importance it places on the capital account of the balance of payments. With financial capital assumed to flow freely among countries in search of the highest interest rate, a change in domestic interest rates (through monetary or fiscal policy) will induce a capital flow that moves the exchange rate to offset any disequilibrium in a country's external position which would have resulted from the policy change. Various permutations of the Mundell-Fleming model can be used to show under which circumstances (for instance, fixed or floating exchange rates; free or zero capital mobility) a government's attempts to influence domestic prices and incomes through monetary and fiscal policy will be more and less successful. For example, in the case of perfect capital mobility and fixed exchange rates – as in, say, a small EMS country – a monetary expansion is immediately reversed through a capital outflow. With floating rates, monetary expansion will cause a currency depreciation and an increase in nominal income – which may mean inflation, if resources are already fully employed, or an increase in real income if there was slack in the economy.

The beauty of the Mundell-Fleming model is the clarity and flexibility of its framework. But as experience with floating rates accumulated in the mid-1970s, concerns about the consequences of capital mobility began to surface. Floating rates did *not* seem to insulate governments from the effects of one another's policies by allowing the strain to be taken in the exchange rate. Capital did *not* seem to move purely on the basis of interest rate differentials, but showed a distressing tendency to surge towards currencies that were expected to appreciate, thereby aggravating exchange rate movements. Numerous models and theories have appeared in the last 15 years to account for the unexpected difficulties encountered in practice with the floating rate system. Some of these build on the Mundell-Fleming framework by incorporating *expectations* about future exchange rate movements into the interest rate equation (Dornbusch, 1976; Frenkel and Razin, 1987). More recent work has tended to focus on explaining particular observed phenomena in the behaviour of exchange rates such as overshooting and speculative bubbles.

To summarize, in the field of international finance the economics profession has built up a solid core of established theory about the behaviour of economies and their linkages under both fixed and floating exchange rate regimes. But experience over the period since the breakdown of Bretton Woods in 1972 has gradually eroded the consensus that had been reached over the superiority of a floating rate system as a means of managing economic linkages among countries. The noted American economist Peter Kenen has summed up the current state of thinking thus:

Events and research in the 1980s have undermined the earlier consensus but have not produced a new one. For some, they proved that foreign exchange markets are inefficient and even irrational; the run-up of the US dollar in 1983–85 is described as a 'speculative bubble' that defied the fundamentals. For others, they proved something less startling; the reduction and convergence of inflation rates is far from sufficient for achieving exchange-rate stability. But there is, I believe, a large measure of agreement on another point: that the costs of floating have been very high. Floating exchange rates cannot reduce inter-dependence, but can only change its form. They may indeed produce a peculiarly painful form in a world where prices and wages are sticky, so that changes in nominal exchange rates are matched almost fully by changes in real exchange rates. Under these conditions, exchange-rate stability becomes an objective in its own right, not an incidental reward for following sound policies. (Kenen, 1988)

Given the turmoil in foreign exchange markets of the last decade, a new consensus seems to be growing around Kenen and others for a return to a fixed-but-adjustable or crawling peg system (Kenen, 1988; Bergsten, 1988). It is argued in Chapter 4 that, in a world where foreign-owned firms are a more important vehicle than trade for the integration of markets for goods and services, exchange rates are a less powerful tool for economic management. Misalignment will matter less and trade imbalances will be less susceptible to correction via changes in exchange rates. Because they have lost much of their 'grounding' as a price that equilibrates real flows of goods and services, exchange rates are also likely to be more volatile. Under such conditions, a global 'target zone' system would give undue importance to the exchange rate – and, indirectly, to trade imbalances – as the key variable for policy coordination.

On a regional basis, however, the costs and benefits of exchange rate targeting can look quite different. For a medium-sized country such as Britain, there can be great advantage in integrating its monetary policy with those of its closest economic partners through a jointly managed exchange rate system. If exchange rates are becoming both less powerful as a policy instrument and, at the same time, more volatile, then a smaller country can reduce exchange rate uncertainty for its businesses and consumers while losing little scope in economic management by linking its currency to that of a larger trading bloc. If, in addition, that bloc is intensifying its internal economic integration (aiming at becoming a single market by 1992), then the costs of exchange rate linkage are further reduced.

In a world where global companies weave a network of economic linkages that reach directly into one another's economies, policy coordination among governments will indeed be necessary. But Chapter 5 argues that it can more usefully be focused on an expanding agenda of microeconomic issues, such as financial market regulation, competition policy, consumer protection and environmental standards. These will affect macroeconomic outcomes such as growth and trade through their impact on business decisions and the 'levelling of playing fields'. In such an integrating but complex world economy, the proposal by some economists 'to view the whole range of domestic economic policies, macro and micro, through the lens of the exchange rate' (Bergsten, 1988) seems unnecessarily to remove an important degree of freedom. By contrast, this paper suggests that economic growth and integration will be enhanced by *demoting* the role of the exchange rate and the current account balance in international policy discussions and *promoting* the importance of agreed rules for trade, investment and competition in one another's markets.

2

GLOBAL COMPANIES AND THE DIRECT INVESTMENT EXPLOSION

This chapter focuses on outward investment: the cross-border flows that constitute FDI. While world trade volumes grew at a compound annual rate of 5% between 1983 and 1988, global FDI increased by over 20% per annum in real terms over that period. Yet FDI flows are only a partial measure of the fundamental restructuring of ownership and competition patterns that is taking place in the advanced economies. Chapter 3 looks at inward investment and broadens the analysis to examine the total impact of foreign-owned firms – whether financed through cross-border flows or domestically – on their host economies. Together, these two chapters lay the groundwork for the discussion in Chapter 4 of the relationship between investment and trade flows, and what they imply for the analysis of economic interdependence among nations.

Definitions, data and scope of analysis

The terminology surrounding the phenomena of international investment is often used imprecisely and is thus subject to confusion. In addition there are numerous problems with the actual data, particularly when comparing figures from different countries. This makes it risky to embark on a detailed statistical search for explanatory patterns. Even if one should be discovered, no great confidence could be placed in it.

Nonetheless, in many respects the FDI figures are no worse than trade data available to economists. Very rarely does one find that

Country A's recorded exports to Country B come within 10% of Country B's recorded imports from Country A for the same period. The great 'black hole' in the world's aggregate balance of payments – which implies that the world is in deficit with itself to the tune of between $50 billion and $100 billion per year – is well-known. The difference is that for trade figures international reference sources have been developed (examples being the GATT, the IMF, the UN) which have removed some of the obvious definitional discrepancies and which, more importantly, have become authoritative sources in their own right, although they include pages of health warnings about the data they contain. Although the UN and the OECD collate data on FDI, they do not correct it for definitional differences between countries, and they publish with a considerable lag. It is only possible to obtain up-to-date and disaggregated data on FDI from national sources. The main sources of error introduced into cross-country analysis by differing definitions are discussed below.

Before proceeding to the data, however, it is important to be clear about what is and what is not included in the general definition of FDI. The most widely accepted definition is that provided by the IMF:

> direct investment refers to investment that is made to acquire a lasting interest in an enterprise operating in an economy other than that of the investor, the investor's purpose being to have an effective voice in the management of the enterprise. (IMF, 1977)

This definition focuses on the key *motivational* aspect that distinguishes direct investment from portfolio investment. The latter, by analogy, is motivated by a passive, and possibly fleeting, interest in acquiring the interest, dividends or capital gains of the investment, without any say in its management. The IMF definition says nothing about the extent of ownership required for an investment to be considered direct, and neither does it state whether a distinction should be made between the takeover of an existing enterprise and the creation of a new 'greenfield' company. It does not distinguish between investments financed by borrowing in the host country capital market and those involving a transfer of funds internationally from the parent to the subsidiary. And, since government

15

statistical offices cannot measure the motivational rationale for direct investment and, unlike trade flows, foreign direct investment passes through no customs points, it has been necessary to augment the IMF definition with a few rules of thumb.

In 1982, in order to standardize data collection across countries, the OECD suggested that 10% ownership of the voting stock of an enterprise should be considered 'a lasting interest'. In fact, most FDI is associated with ownership shares in excess of 50% and survey evidence suggests that 100% ownership is still the norm for US and Japanese overseas investment. Thus the fact that the UK and France use a 20% minimum rule in their FDI statistics, while Germany uses 25% and the US and Japan abide by the OECD guideline, is an annoying, but not overwhelming, obstacle to cross-country comparisons and aggregations.

In addition to this statistical clarification as to what constitutes 'a lasting interest' it has been necessary for some purposes to distinguish between FDI that is locally financed and that which creates a cross-border flow of funds. Clearly, the latter is included in balance-of-payments measures, while the former is not – except, as noted below, for an increase in the value of the subsidiary through its retained earnings. The most reliable and up-to-date statistics on FDI are collected on a balance-of-payments basis. These are reasonably comparable across countries and they show the total size of FDI flows, whether for minority ownership stakes in existing firms or for new greenfield plants. Most of the discussion in this paper, except in Chapter 3, is based on such data.

The disadvantage of balance-of-payments data is that they do not provide sufficient disaggregation of flows; for example, the composition of FDI by sector, country of origin, size of foreign ownership stake, share of domestic production or employment, or link to trade data. For such information, one must rely on surveys carried out every three to five years by most countries and on 'notification' data provided by foreign companies to some host governments, notably Japan, on their intentions (which generally far overstate actual flows). Chapter 3 uses such data when it refers to measures of foreign-owned-firm (FOF) importance.

The lower part of Figure 2.1 shows how the data from balance-of-payments sources and surveys are related to the concepts of FDI and FOF measures (the top part of the figure is discussed later in this chapter). Because FDI is a balance-of-payments measure, the

Figure 2.1 Schematic of FDI and FOF measures

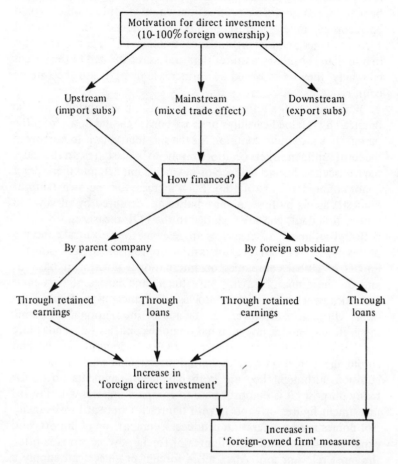

method of its financing is relevant. If the finance comes from the (foreign) parent company, regardless of whether the parent uses its retained earnings or raises new money through bank loans or equity issues, a capital flow crosses the border and it is classified as FDI. In addition, the domestically financed expansion of a foreign subsidiary through its retained earnings (via internal cash generation) is included in FDI for most countries even though no actual cross-border movement of funds has taken place. To understand the rationale for this, consider the alternative. If, instead of expanding its foreign operations through investing its profits locally, the foreign subsidiary repatriated those profits through a dividend flow back to the parent, then a reverse flow would take place which would be recorded under 'interest, profits and dividends' in the current account. Thus a consistent statistical treatment of retained earnings in a foreign subsidiary requires that, unless repatriated to the parent company, they be recorded as an increase in FDI into the foreign country.

Of course, not all foreign acquisitions or expansions will be financed by retained earnings or cross-border capital flows from the parent. It is also quite common for the subsidiary itself to borrow in the local capital markets or, more rarely, to issue shares. In this case, the transaction has no balance-of-payments impact, and therefore it is not counted as part of FDI. Such increases in the ownership of domestic assets by foreign subsidiaries are captured by survey and notification data, and are included in the FOF measures.

Both FDI and FOF measures are relevant to the central concerns of this paper. The FDI measure is more appropriate for assessing the impact of global companies on international investment patterns and on the domestic savings/investment imbalances of particular countries which manifest themselves in balance-of-payments positions. Ultimately, however, the degree of international economic integration – and the impact it has on public policies – depends more on the accumulating importance of FOFs in domestic output and employment than on how the initial investments were financed. In addition, although they are both balance-of-payments flows, for many purposes it is inappropriate to compare imports with inward investment figures or exports with figures for outward investment. For domestic consumers and producers, comparison of imports and exports with the local sales figures of foreign-owned firms is often the most relevant test. After all, a foreign producer can supply a domestic consumer either by exporting or by selling directly from its domestically established subsidiary. It is not the *investment* in that subsidiary that is the relevant measure, but its sales. This distinction is brought out in more detail in Chapter 4 where the relationship between trade and investment is explored.

There are two particular problems with the cross-country compatibility of data on FDI (balance-of-payments basis) from the G-5 countries. The first concerns the treatment of retained earnings, these being the profits of a foreign subsidiary which are held within the company rather than paid as dividends back to the parent. Figure 2.1 is based on the OECD suggestion that retained earnings be included in FDI. This suggestion is adhered to by the US, Britain and Germany; but not by France or Japan. Thus a profitable subsidiary of a British firm operating in the US which used all or part of its profits to expand its US business would cause a recorded increase in British FDI into the US although no funds actually crossed the border. In recent years these retained earnings have been quite significant. For example, according to US data, the retained earnings of Japanese companies in the US amounted to nearly one-third of total Japanese FDI flows to the US during the 1980s. Since Japan is the fastest growing international investor, its failure to include retained earnings in its data will rapidly undermine the validity of international comparisons and aggregates.

The second major problem with the data on FDI is that investments are carried at their 'book' value (which is generally their initial cost) and are not revalued over time to reflect increases in their actual worth – which is what they would fetch in the marketplace. Thus for each country the figures for the *stock* of foreign direct investment assets are understated, and this problem is especially serious for those countries with long histories of foreign investment such as Britain and the United States. A further difficulty is that some countries – notably France and Japan – do not publish figures on their total stock of foreign direct investment assets. It is possible, of course, to add up the year-by-year flows of their FDI to arrive at an idea of the total outstanding stock, but this presents an incomplete picture unless retained earnings and increases in the value of existing assets are recorded.

There are various other problems that affect all countries' data: inflation and exchange rate movements over time, loans and repayments between parent companies and foreign affiliates, the treatment of investment in Country A by a firm in Country B whose parent company is resident in Country C, etc. Such problems with data and definitions are multiplying as the activities of global companies proliferate. It is not surprising, therefore, that detailed sectoral or bilateral breakdowns of FDI flows often appear erratic and are difficult to interpret. Beyond identifying the obvious differences and making adjustments where possible, the approach taken in this paper is to rely mostly on aggregate figures across sectors, on home-currency data for each country and on inflation-adjusted comparisons over time. The appendix describes the sources used and data adjustments made for each country.

Although each country's data on FDI contain definitional quirks, and there is no international reference for FDI data comparable to the GATT data on trade flows or the IMF data on balance-of-payments accounts, the concentration of the flows themselves makes it possible to analyse trends from national data sources. Two-thirds of the total world stock of FDI is held by just three countries: the United States, Great Britain and Japan. The research on which this paper is based also includes the Federal Republic of Germany and France. This group of five countries (the G-5) corresponds to the core membership of the economic summit team that tries to coordinate macroeconomic policies. The inclusion of these two additional European countries also provides a better base for future work if indications are borne out that Western Europe will be the most active field for FDI flows over the next few years. This five-country sample accounts for more than three-quarters of the total stock of foreign assets held by the OECD countries.

An overview of the 1980s
It is useful to set the development of G-5 FDI during the 1980s into its broader historical and geographical context. Figure 2.2 shows annual aggregate flows of FDI into and out of the G-5 since 1961. The wave pattern of surges and retrenchments is evident at this aggregate level, as are the extreme heights that have been reached in the last few years.

The pattern of FDI in the 1980s is one of strong and sustained recovery after a fall in the early part of the decade due to worldwide recession and the aftermath of the second oil shock. In real terms,* FDI outflows from the G-5 in 1988 were nearly 40% above their previous peak of 1979. As shown in Table 2.1, the United States and Britain – the world's largest direct investors – have recorded increases in real terms of over 15% per year over the past five years. Japan and France, starting from much lower bases, have increased their FDI at more than 30% per year.

Figure 2.2 also illustrates the relationship between inflows and outflows of FDI among the G-5. Over the whole period since 1961,

*All real, or inflation-adjusted, figures in this paper are based on 1980 prices.

Figure 2.2   Aggregate outflows/inflows of FDI by the G-5 (US $ bn)

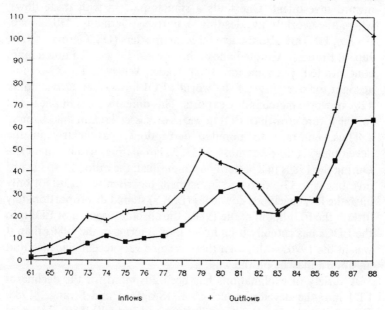

■ Inflows   + Outflows

Table 2.1 FDI outflows by the G-5
(compound annual growth rates, valued in domestic currency)

	FDI flows 1983–8		FDI stock* 1988
	Nominal (%)	Real (%)	($ bn)
United States	24	20	324
United Kingdom	22	16	184
Japan	39	37	114
Germany	18	15	78
France	39	32	57

*For consistency across countries, the stock is taken to be the cumulative FDI outflow over the period 1961–88.

FDI into the G-5 countries (from all sources) has amounted to over half of the FDI they provided to the rest of the world. In other words, these five countries are not only major outward investors,

21

they are also (with the exception of Japan) major recipients of inward investment. One finds a similar pattern with trade flows, where the world's five leading exporters (Germany, US, Japan, France, UK) are also the five largest importers (US, Germany, UK, Japan, France). As noted above, however, FDI is still a much more concentrated phenomenon than trade. Whereas the G-5 now account for over 75% of the world's FDI flows, they provide only 42% of world merchandise exports. This difference has implications for the future growth of FDI flows, as discussed later in this chapter.

Thus, contrary to popular perceptions, particularly in the developing countries, most FDI is circulating within the G-5. During the 1980s this pattern has intensified; the ratio of G-5 inward investment to G-5 outward investment has risen to 0.75. Not only have the less developed countries (LDCs) shared disproportionately little in the FDI boom of the 1980s, the absolute amount of FDI into the LDCs has actually been lower in real terms in the 1980s than it was in the 1970s – although there is some very recent evidence that an upturn may be on the way.

A variety of explanations has been advanced for the decline of FDI into the developing countries (Stopford and Strange, 1988; Riedel, Büttner and Ernst, 1988; Page and Riddell, 1989). The debt problems of the Latin American countries have stifled investment, both directly by increasing the risk for investors that they will be unable to repatriate profits in foreign currency and indirectly by reducing the growth rates of domestic demand in those economies. Many African countries have suffered declines in per capita income that make them less attractive sites for investment. Excess capacity in world commodity markets and weak commodity prices have combined to depress international investment in a sector which is traditionally important for developing countries.

It is ironic that the policy climate for inward investment has actually improved in many of the LDCs during the last five years, while the inflows themselves have declined. There seems to be a growing recognition by the developing countries – strongly prompted, it must be said, by the World Bank – that FDI can be an attractive vehicle for the transfer both of financial resources and of technology. However, many of the policy changes towards FDI implemented in the LDCs address the problems of the 1970s rather than the opportunities of the 1980s. As discussed later in this chapter, the biggest growth area for FDI in the 1980s has been in the service sectors (such as banking, insurance, transport, telecommunications), where the LDCs' economies are still riddled with restrictions, price distortions and public monopolies.

A major exception to the disappointing trend of falling FDI into the developing countries is the East Asian area. Both the newly industrializing economies (NIEs) – Korea, Taiwan, Singapore and Hong Kong – and the ASEAN countries – which, in addition to Singapore, include Thailand, Malaysia, Indonesia, Brunei and the Philippines – have achieved remarkably high rates of economic growth during the 1980s. Korea and Taiwan have liberalized their historically restrictive policies towards inward investment, while Hong Kong and Singapore have long courted foreign capital. This policy stance, coupled with their proximity to Japan – the fastest growing international investor – has led to a major expansion of FDI flows into the area in recent years.

With a few notable exceptions, then, the upsurge of FDI in the 1980s has come from and gone into the OECD countries. Within this group, however, there has been a major shift in direction and increase in dispersion of flows since the 1960s. These developments broadly reflect the underlying changes in the world economy. Between 1960 and 1975 only the United States was a significant *net* exporter of FDI. Its net outflows (i.e., US FDI outflows less inflows into the US) reached 79% of the total G-5 outflows in 1966. Britain and Japan were also net outward investors during this period, but in amounts that paled in comparison with those of the US. France and Germany were net importers of FDI.

After the dramatic jump in prices of oil and other commodities in 1973, all of the G-5 countries except France became large net exporters of FDI. This reflected their desire to secure supplies of oil and certain other raw materials, and also showed the enhanced profitability of investment in energy resources. The international oil companies were already major foreign investors, and they were able to respond quickly to the stimulus for increased investment brought about by the fourfold increase in international oil prices.

By 1980 the commodity price boom had peaked and its effects had sown the seeds of the world recession that took hold with a vengeance in 1981. That was also the year when the earlier trends in FDI flows by the G-5 culminated in a reversal of net flows for the

United States. For the first time in many decades, the US experienced a net *inflow* of FDI. It has been a net recipient ever since, although in most years it remains the largest FDI exporter.

At the same time as the US became a net recipient of FDI, France reversed its net position and has been a net FDI exporter for six of the last seven years. In 1985 Japan became the largest net direct investor, followed by the UK and Germany. As discussed below, Japan's rapid rise to this position is due to a combination of rapidly growing outflows and negligible inflows.

The rest of this chapter and the next examine the sources and destinations of these FDI flows separately and in more detail for the period of the 1980s. This exercise is necessary in order to understand the forces behind the massive increase in FDI flows at the aggregate level. However, it is essential to keep in mind the two-way nature of this international transaction. The popular debate over FDI too often focuses on allegations that outward FDI exports jobs that could otherwise be created at home, or that inward FDI represents the surrender of domestic industry to foreign control. In addition to the internal contradiction in these views, they demonstrate a zero-sum mentality that comes from focusing on one element of a transaction that is part of a much larger picture. As Adam Smith first demonstrated with trade flows, both the sending and the receiving countries benefit from such voluntary exchange, although individual companies in either country may be hurt. Indeed, it would be impossible to reap the benefits of more efficient production and lower prices to consumers if the less efficient were not displaced, thereby releasing labour and capital for expansion in the more efficient sectors. Neither trade nor international investment is a zero-sum game, although focusing on only half of the story often leads to that misperception. The mercantilist fallacy has yet to be expunged from the foreign investment debate.

Outward investment: who is making it and why?
There are two main approaches to answering this question. The first is to focus on the microeconomic, or firm-level, decision to invest in a foreign country. Many volumes have been written on this – by economists, business school professors and political scientists – and many useful insights have been gained although no general theory has emerged. Such research generally relies on interviews and case

studies of individual firms or on surveys of firm-level financial and production data.

The second approach – the one taken in this paper – is to look for the macroeconomic and political factors that have shaped the business environment against which firms make their individual decisions. This approach requires an empirical basis which extends both across time (for the macroeconomic factors) and across countries (for the political ones). There are few examples of this approach in the literature, perhaps because data collection is arduous and political comparisons are necessarily inexact. The number of excellent one-country studies employing a macroeconomic approach is growing, but they run the risk of attributing causation to national economic or political changes that, in fact, are part of larger international trends (on Germany, von Pfeil 1985; on the US, Graham and Krugman, 1989).

The micro and the macro approaches are clearly complementary; each can yield insights for the other. Thus, before discussing the macroeconomic results of this study, it is useful to summarize some of the key findings from the literature on firm-level foreign investment decisions. For a more complete survey see Chapter 1 of Casson (1987) or Thomsen (1990).

Microeconomic explanations
The pioneering work on MNEs was by Kindleberger (1969) and his student Hymer (1976) at MIT in the 1960s. They were essentially asking the question 'How is it possible for a foreign firm to compete successfully with indigenous firms when it faces the extra costs of acclimatizing to the foreign business environment?' Their answer, which also drew on British economist John Dunning's pioneering study of US FDI in Britain (Dunning, 1958), was that the foreign firm often had advantages of a monopolistic or monopsonistic type, sometimes deriving from superior technology or management skills. Some of these anti-competitive advantages stemmed from market failures (especially in the licensing of technology) or from high transaction costs in moving goods or factors between countries.

In the 1970s a number of writers developed the latter idea by asking 'Why are plants in different countries brought under common control?' and answering 'Because the transaction costs incurred in intermediate products markets can be reduced by internalizing these markets within the firm' (McManus, 1972; Buckley and

Casson, 1976). This idea of reducing costs through internalizing markets, both for inputs and for the distribution of outputs, is the basic rationale for the horizontal integration of firms. Standard models of horizontal integration (an example being Horst, 1971) explain multi-plant operations as such, without reference to an international dimension. Indeed, based on this theory only, one might expect that most MNEs would come from small economies where multi-plant internalization could be achieved only by looking abroad. Except in particular sectors such as oil, it is hard to explain the dominance of US MNEs with a theory of market internalization.

A number of theories have been advanced to explain the vertical integration of firms (again, not necessarily across borders). Here the question is 'Under what circumstances is it profitable for a firm to link its upstream activities (such as procuring inputs) with its production activities and with its sales (or exporting) activities?' This kind of question is useful for understanding the linkages between trade and investment, and for explaining why it is impossible to generalize about the impact of an increase in FDI flows on either the size or the net direction of a country's trade flows.

Refer to the top part of Figure 2.1 and consider the example of a British clothing company which imports cotton fabric from Egypt, manufactures dresses in Britain, sells domestically and exports to the United States. As described, this company is responsible for no FDI, but it imports some of its inputs and exports some of its outputs. Now suppose it begins to have trouble with the reliability of deliveries of cotton cloth from Egypt. It suspects its Egyptian supplier is not giving its orders the priority it would like. The British firm decides to buy out the supplier and run the Egyptian plant as a subsidiary. This is upstream vertical integration which occurs through an FDI flow from the UK to Egypt. From the company's point of view, the investment has substituted for imports by inter-nalizing the procurement of inputs that were previously purchased. However, the volume of trade flows between the two countries is unaffected; the value of the trade may go down depending on the internal transfer price that the company decides to use in valuing the cotton cloth. (For tax reasons, this transfer price cannot be too far from what it would have been as an 'arm's length transaction', but there is usually some scope for varying the transfer price depending on where the company chooses to keep its profits.)

Next suppose that demand in the US for the company's output is so strong that the company decides to set up its own chain of retail outlets (as, for example, Laura Ashley has done). This is down-stream vertical integration which internalizes the export flow from the company's point of view. It is accomplished by an FDI flow from the UK to the US and by continued (but now intra-firm) trade between the two countries.

Having gained experience operating in two new markets, the company may now decide to move some of its basic production processes upstream to Egypt (where labour costs are lower than in Britain) and some downstream to the United States (for fashion items where quick response to shifts in market tastes is critical). FDI flows will again be generated by this mainstream FDI. In addition, there will be a fall in Britain's GDP, in British imports from Egypt and in British exports to the US (in the first instance, assuming the demand is unchanged). Egyptian exports to the US will be increased. Meanwhile, assuming profit expectations were realized, the British parent will have reaped the gains of vertical integration through cost savings and better marketing. If it repatriates some of these increased profits, Britain's current account deficit will be reduced.

This simple example illustrates the complexity of FDI–trade linkages even for a one-company case over time. An economy-wide aggregation, involving companies in different sectors and at different points in their integration strategies, is nothing more than that: an aggregation. The fact that during some periods, in some countries, increased FDI inflows have led to a worsening of the trade balance should be interpreted as an empirical finding with little explanatory or predictive significance.

Theories on vertical integration try to explain the increase in FDI over time by noting that there have been changes in technical, market power and fiscal factors which have increased the benefits of vertical integration. On the technical side they point to high fixed costs caused by heavy capital intensity (for instance, in automobiles) or the need for high levels of research expenditures which have to be recouped quickly through global sales (Ohmae, 1985). Market power factors include negative features such as trade restrictions and barriers to entry in service markets, as well as positive features such as the need to have a 'local presence' in some industries in order to be taken seriously by potential customers. Fiscal factors relate to incentives for creative transfer pricing caused by different tax regimes in the home and host countries.

27

Figure 2.3   FDI outflows from the G-5, by country (US $ bn)

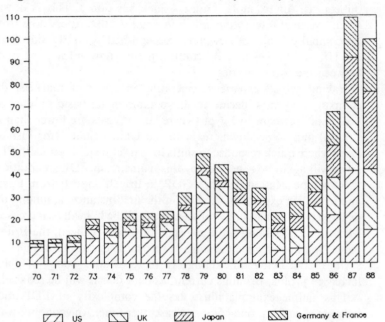

The microeconomic literature on the motivations for FDI has produced a large range of plausible (and empirically documented) explanations. All of these undoubtedly apply to certain companies in certain sectors at certain points in time. Surveys of multinational companies have also been undertaken which have revealed a wide spread of motives for foreign investments, with most respondents listing more than one reason (Group of Thirty, 1984). As with the decision to enter a foreign market via export, so with FDI the case will rest both on the particular situation of competitors in that market and on the set of alternative opportunities available to the potential exporter in that and other markets. Beyond that rather obvious generalization, it is difficult to distil robust explanatory patterns from the microeconomic literature.

Macroeconomic patterns
We have already seen in Table 2.1 that all of the G-5 countries contributed to the rapid increase in FDI flows since 1983. Figure 2.3 illustrates the country composition of G-5 FDI since 1970.

Individual country data show a striking similarity of pattern over an even longer period, with outward flows peaking around 1973 and 1979–80, then plummeting during the oil shocks to reach nadirs in 1974 and 1982–3.

These years of FDI peaks and valleys coincide with trends in economic growth and recession in the advanced economies. The correlation between real FDI growth and real GNP growth can be tested statistically. Using aggregate data for the five countries over the 25-year period 1963–88 inclusive, the following regression equation is fitted:*

$$FDI = -0.06 + 3.44 \; GNP$$
$$(-0.33) \quad (5.23)$$

Where FDI = percent change in real FDI by the G-5
GNP = percent change in real GNP of the G-5

This equation suggests that a 1% increase (decrease) in real GNP coincides with a 3.4% increase (decrease) in real FDI. In other words, FDI growth mirrors GNP growth but has increased over three times as fast since the early 1960s. When the same regression is run separately for two sub-periods, the GNP coefficient increases from 3.01 in 1963–79 to 3.65 in 1979–88, a statistically significant change. This reflects the stronger upsurge in FDI, relative to the growth of income, during this decade.

Using aggregate data from the five countries together produces a better result than running individual equations for each country. The aggregation diminishes the effect of a random occurrence in an individual country in a given year. In addition, because these five countries are also the major recipients of FDI, the use of aggregated GNP as the independent variable captures the importance of both the home and the host economy in the investment decision. While slow growth in the host country erodes investment opportunities, the same slow growth at home impairs business optimism and the ability of parent companies to raise funds for FDI. Because of the global nature of booms and recessions in recent years, the idea that FDI would be 'drawn out' or 'sucked back' by *differentials* in growth rates between host and home countries was not supported by the statistical tests. The more likely explanation is that trends in both economic growth and foreign direct investment are now global phenomena, at least among the major OECD countries.

*T statistics are shown in parentheses. The correlation coefficient, R squared, is 0.53.

It is clear that the strong economic growth we have enjoyed since the early 1980s has provided an important macroeconomic stimulus for the FDI surge. One must also consider changes in the political environment. The two that are most often cited in the popular press – the 1992 process of creating a single market in Europe and the fear of protectionism, especially in the US – while undoubtedly of some importance, do not seem to be the dominant driving forces.

Agreement on the 1992 objectives was reached in 1985, but it took some time after the programme was agreed for most European countries to recognize its significance, and even longer for the Americans and Japanese to do so. The FDI surge got under way in 1983–4. Furthermore, it was the United States, rather than the EC countries, that saw the fastest growth in inward investment. There are some signs in the very recent data that intra-EC flows of FDI may now be growing faster than flows from the EC and Japan into the US, as predicted in earlier work (Julius and Thomsen, 1988). Looking ahead, the 1992 initiative is expected to provide an important political stimulus to FDI into Europe during the early 1990s, but this will be against the backdrop of the much larger, sustained increase in global FDI that began in the early 1980s for other reasons and predominantly in other regions.

The second frequently cited political rationale for direct investment is the fear of protectionism. There is no doubt that this has been and remains *one* important motivation for Japanese direct investment into both the US and Europe. Again, however, the overall pattern of the FDI data does not support the hypothesis that the increased fear of trade restraints has been the *dominant* explanation of the FDI growth during the 1980s. The fastest growing areas for FDI have been the service sectors where the trade and investment climate has actually become more open and market-oriented. The British have been a bigger investor into the US than the Japanese, although there are no voluntary export restraints (VERs) on UK goods in the US. Even for the Japanese, whose history of VERs and trade disputes with the US goes back at least two decades, it is hard to believe that the protectionist worries of the 1980s have been so much worse than those of earlier periods that they could account for the eightfold increase of Japanese FDI in the US that occurred between 1980 and 1988.

An examination of the cross-country and cross-sector data suggests that two other changes in the regulatory and policy environment have been particularly important in stimulating FDI flows. The first is the liberalization and deregulation of the service sectors that began in the United States and has now spread throughout the G-5; and the second is the complex of political and economic changes ignited in Japan by the sudden emergence of its large current account surplus.

Wall Street's 'big bang' in 1975 set off a financial revolution that caused other world centres to rethink their regulations, especially those regarding foreign competition in securities markets which had been reserved almost universally for nationals. The emergence of large financial conglomerates in the US (examples being American Express and Merrill Lynch) put pressure on national competition elsewhere and this in turn brought a wave of liberalization that is still spreading. It is instructive that such liberalization has resulted in more, rather than less, competition in national markets, as Nomura and Daiwa, for example, emerged from Japan to challenge the US financial giants on their home ground. Paradoxically, the *removal* of regulations that had been instigated partly to guard against national monopolistic tendencies led to an *increase* in competition, and a reduction in prices for consumers, in the domestic market.

An example from another large service sector is the US anti-trust case of 1984 which led to the dismemberment of its monopoly telecommunications supplier, AT&T. This has had two major impacts. First, it has served as a model and impetus for countries such as the UK and Japan which also wanted to stimulate a sector that had traditionally been a public monopoly. Second, the rump AT&T company has been galvanized into becoming a global player by building strategic alliances with competitors around the world. This has meant that even the most illiberal telecommunications monopolies elsewhere have been confronted with the new fact of global competition. They too are having to devise international strategies to come to terms with the underlying forces now shaping the industry.

Just as, in the 1970s, the driving force for FDI growth was the oil sector, so in the 1980s it has been the service sector. Table 2.2 shows that for the three major outward investors FDI in services grew faster than total FDI over the period 1980–8. In looking to the future, however, there is a fundamental difference between oil-inspired FDI and service-driven flows. The oil industry has long been vertically integrated, it is mature in structure, and thus FDI

31

Table 2.2 The share of services in total outward FDI
(% of total stock)

	1980	1988	Change
Japan	25	58	33
US	33	41	8
UK	38	39	1
Germany	31	31	0
France	44	40	−4

flows are price-responsive rather than structurally driven. They can be expected to go down as oil prices fall – which is indeed what has happened in the 1980s. By contrast, there are service industries in many countries that are still heavily regulated and fragmented. Insurance at the retail level is a case in point. In the US each state has its own regulatory authority. In France a local presence is required to sell policies to households. In Japan new products have to be approved before they can be marketed. Yet there are clearly economies of scale in the risk-spreading business of insurance, and there are large price and product differences among countries.

A crack has begun to open in the regulatory structures that have protected many service industries behind national borders. This crack is certain to open further, albeit slowly and with setbacks as well as advances. Foreign direct investment will push its way through, bringing major changes in industry structure and linking formerly separate national markets as a result.

If the deregulation trend continues and spreads to other countries, as is the explicit intent both of the 1992 process and of the GATT negotiations, the scope for future expansion of FDI and trade in the service sectors could be very large. Table 2.3 shows the importance of services to various economic aggregates for the US and the UK. Predictably, the external measures such as trade and investment lag far behind the domestic measures such as output and employment. Because of the nature of services, many of which cannot be traded directly because they require contact between the buyer and the seller, it is likely that services will always be a smaller fraction of exports and imports than they are of domestic production or consumption (Nicolaides, 1989). But no similar rationale applies to investment. Precisely because services such as hotels and catering

Table 2.3 The importance of services to the US and to the UK (% of total represented by services)

	US	UK
Labour force	73	68
GNP	70	56
Exports*	20	25
Imports*	14	23
Outward FDI†	41	39
Inward FDI†	53	25

Note: Figures are for various dates from 1984 to 1988.
*Includes only non-factor services.
†These shares are by industry of affiliate. Because some FDI involves sales affiliates set up by manufacturing firms, the share of services in FDI by industry of the parent would be lower.

cannot be traded, the only way for a hotel chain to reach a foreign market is to invest there. Only then can consumers of local hotel services avail themselves of potentially better or cheaper service from a foreign rival. (If the foreign company did not think it could provide this, it would not have made the investment.) Thus much of the investment in the service sector is driven by exactly the same motivation – and is beneficial to both sides for exactly the same reason – as trade flows.

Along with service sector deregulation, the other political–economic shift that has been a major stimulus to FDI during the 1980s has been the rather sudden emergence of the current account surplus in Japan. This has set in motion both economic and political forces that have combined to create a powerful impetus for Japanese companies to shift and expand their operations overseas. The 40% rise in the yen during 1985–7 provided a strong economic incentive for Japan's export-oriented industries to establish overseas production bases both in the country of the final market and in third countries with production costs that were suddenly much lower than those in Japan.

The political impetus came from the Japanese government as it tried to devise economic strategies to defuse the trade tensions that arose from the current account surplus. Seemingly overnight – in the view of many Japanese as well as of Americans and Europeans –

Japan had developed into an economic superpower for whom the standards of behaviour are much stricter than those for a Korea or a Switzerland. The steady stream of exhortation since the end of World War II from the Japanese Economic Planning Agency and the Ministry of Trade and Industry (MITI) to work hard and promote exports in order to catch up with the West was no longer appropriate. Japan no longer fitted the picture of the resource-poor island whose people must export in order to eat. Instead, Japan was perceived as the 'free rider' in the world trade system, taking advantage of the open markets of others while keeping its own tightly closed (Prestowitz, 1988). Worse still, the full range of domestic economic policy was suddenly placed under scrutiny, and found to be wanting by international standards. Japan's system of farm support is grossly trade-distorting, with the highest average subsidy per unit of output of any OECD country – notwithstanding the fact that Japan is also the largest food importer. The system of tax-free interest on postal savings deposits that Japan introduced after the war to encourage household savings is attacked because it has contributed to the savings/investment imbalance that is reflected in the export/import imbalance and because it provides unfair competition to foreign banks now allowed to operate in Japan.

By the mid-1980s it was clear to many in the Japanese government that the country would have to undergo a fundamental restructuring to equip itself for its newly acquired international status and to live up to the standards of behaviour that implied. To circumvent the entrenched bureaucracy, Prime Minister Nakasone established an independent commission, headed by former central bank governor Haruo Maekawa, with a brief to chart new directions for the 1990s. The so-called Maekawa report which resulted from the commission's work recommended a fundamental about-face of the economy from export-led growth to domestic-led demand. Both macroeconomic and microeconomic measures were put forward to achieve this, including the restructuring of Japanese industry toward knowledge-based, higher value-added production, with labour-intensive operations moved offshore. MITI's Industrial Structure Council took up the theme in its 1986 report:

> ... it is very difficult, yet not impossible, ... for Japan to resolve the problem of economic imbalance with other nations in the context of creative growth of the world economy towards the

year 2000. Basic to this is the implementation of macroeconomic policies which emphasize domestic demand, and of an
exchange-rate policy which will stabilize the yen at a high level.
... With these as the basic policy line, an industrial structure
policy aimed at expanding direct overseas investment, promoting imports, and encouraging the transfer of technology should
be implemented. (Industrial Structure Council, 1986)

The net result of these economic and political forces for Japanese
FDI has been to increase its growth rate during the 1980s to more
than double the rate achieved in the 1970s. Furthermore, this rate
has been accelerating in the last few years. Since 1983, Japanese FDI
outflows have virtually doubled every two years (measured in yen),
promoting Japan from seventh place in the league of international
direct investors in 1980 to third place (after the US and the UK) by
1987. An advisory panel to Japan's Ministry of Trade and Industry
predicted that Japan's FDI would grow by 14% annually to the year
2000. That accords with our prediction that Japan will overtake the
UK, in terms of its total FDI stock, in the mid-1990s. Even then, less
than 10% of Japanese companies' production will be carried on
outside Japan (in 1986 it was 4%), compared with 20% for German
firms and 17% for American firms. The 'Japan factor' as a causal
influence on the FDI surge of the 1980s – like the liberalization of
service industries – will be around for some time to come.

The 1990s: will the trend continue?
Neither the aggregate approach taken in this paper nor the available
data lend themselves to econometric projection of future FDI flows.
In addition, the underlying theory provides an eclectic mix of
motivational factors at the firm level which have meaning as an
aggregation but not as separable independent variables. Nonetheless
it is possible to use the qualitative conclusions of the cross-country
analysis of FDI flows to derive a quantitative picture of how global
FDI may plausibly develop. This picture should not be viewed as a
projection for the reasons just mentioned. It simply represents one
'what if' state of the world – a scenario – based on an explicit set of
assumptions whose plausibility derives from the qualitative and
comparative analysis of this chapter.
Three underlying assumptions form the basis of the quantifica-

tion. First, the complex of factors motivating FDI flows is assumed to be similar to those driving trade flows. Although international investment in certain industries and between certain countries has been around for more than a century, as a global phenomenon it is still far less widespread and less deeply rooted than trade. As a means of international economic integration, FDI is in its take-off phase; perhaps in a position comparable to world trade at the end of the 1940s. Post-war economic developments both permitted and were themselves driven by rapidly expanding trade flows. In a similar way, the economic integration of hitherto national markets through FDI, especially in the service industries, can provide a spur to economic growth in the 1990s.

The implication of this assumption for the scenario is that those countries whose industries conduct relatively little of their commercial activities abroad are likely to exhibit more rapid rates of outward FDI growth than those countries whose industries are already well diversified. Parameters such as the stock of outward FDI relative to GNP for the established international investors (the US and the UK) can provide indications of the build-up to be expected from less established investors. Similarly with respect to inward flows – whose 1995 scenario is developed in the next chapter – the situation of the three European countries provides a reference for the newer host economies.

The second and third underlying assumptions relate, respectively, to the international economic and political climate within which FDI takes place. The FDI flows themselves are too volatile year-to-year to make simple extrapolation convincing. Yet over a 25-year period including several business cycles and aggregating the five countries' data, a statistically significant elasticity of 3.44 was obtained, with GNP growth accounting for over 50% of FDI growth. Looking at different sub-periods separately, this elasticity always fell within the range 3.0 to 5.0 and was always statistically significant. While it cannot be applied to individual country cases, as a check on the aggregate scenario figures it would be reasonable to relate this elasticity range to an estimate of GNP growth. The latter is likely to exhibit ups and downs over the seven-year period ending in 1995, but a mainstream prognosis for the average growth rate of GNP in the OECD countries would probably be between 2% and 3% per year. Multiplying this range by that of the FDI/GNP elasticity yields a plausible envelope for the average growth of aggregate FDI (in real terms, i.e., excluding inflation) of between 6% and 15% per year.

Finally, we assume that the political climate surrounding FDI during the period through 1995 will be as open, on average, across countries as it has been during the past decade. In particular, the trend towards liberalization of service industries will spread to additional countries, particularly in Western Europe where it is a central element of the drive to complete the internal market by 1992. The growing public backlash against Japanese FDI in the United States will die down rather than grow as its novelty fades and experience as a host country accumulates. The Japanese government will continue to press for opening of domestic markets, although progress will continue to be slow. In addition, the dramatic political changes in Eastern Europe in 1989 will both allow and provoke new FDI flows in the early 1990s. In short, we assume that as FDI becomes more widespread, with more countries acting as both investors and hosts, public opinion in Europe, the US and Japan will gradually begin to recognize its benefits both for domestic consumers and for the competitiveness of domestic industries. This growing recognition will offset, if it does not supplant, the protectionist pressures that will continue to emanate from the less competitive domestic producers.

The implication of this assumption for the scenario is that FDI will be primarily market-driven, flowing more strongly to those countries which offer greater market potential in terms of both market size and of growth prospects. This implies enhanced flows into the European Community, where effective market size is being expanded by the 1992 process of dismantling barriers, and into Eastern Europe, where buoyant medium-term growth is likely. It also implies continued interest in the US, and selective focus on the LDCs.

From these three underlying assumptions, the scenario for FDI flows through 1995 is built up separately for outward and inward flows from/to the G-5 countries, with the rest of the world (ROW) treated as a separate block. The two sets of flows are matched in a matrix shown at the end of Chapter 3. Regarding outward investment flows, it is clear from the earlier discussion in this chapter that the United States and the United Kingdom have been the most active international investors in the postwar period. There are various measures one might use to compare the depth of their FDI

Table 2.4 Ratios of outward FDI to economic aggregates (%)

	US	UK	Japan	Germany	France
FDI Outflows/Exports					
1961–69	15	6	1.4	2.0	2.4
1970–79	13	10	3.0	2.4	2.2
1980–87	8	14	5.1	2.7	3.9
1995 scenario	10	19	13	6	9
FDI Stock/GNP					
1980	7.3	12	2.3	4.9	2.7
1987	6.9	22	4.8	8.0	5.0
1995 scenario	9.8	50	7.9	15.1	15.2

involvement with the size of their economies; two of these are shown in Table 2.4. The first relates average FDI outflows to average exports, roughly over the three decades since 1960. (Using multi-year averages for FDI avoids the problem of large year-to-year fluctuations caused by lumpy investments in the underlying figures.) These show the relative decline in the US FDI/export ratio after the very high levels reached in the 1960s, as well as the build-up in UK flows to a ratio over the 1980s that was as high, relative to its exports, as that of the US in the 1960s.

By contrast, the ratio of FDI to exports for Japan is only one-third that of the UK for the 1980–7 period, although it is undoubtedly still growing. In domestic currency (which is how these ratios are calculated), Japan's exports have been almost flat over the past three years while FDI has been growing strongly. France and Germany also record increasing ratios of FDI to exports, but at levels still far below that of the UK in the 1960s. There is much scope for further increase.

The second part of Table 2.4 shows the total stock of each country's outward FDI relative to its GNP in 1980 and in 1987. By using FDI stock figures rather than flows, these ratios better reflect the historical dimension of each country's situation. For example, Germany and France have higher ratios than Japan because of their sustained investment patterns over time; Japan now invests much more than either of them but it is still a relative newcomer to the

Table 2.5 Scenario of outward FDI flows and stock to 1995 (billion 1988 US $)

	Av. ann. FDI outflow 1986–8	Av. ann. growth 1988–95† %	FDI outflow 1995	FDI stock 1995	Av. ann. stock growth 1988–95 %
US	27.2	5	38.3	560	8.0
UK	24.3	5	34.2	390	11.5
Japan	22.7	15	60.4	430	19.8
Germany	9.7	10	18.9	179	12.7
France	8.7	10	16.9	147	14.7
ROW	30.9*	10	60.1	574	12.5
Total	123.4*	9.2	228.8	2253	12.1

*Estimate based on assumption that G-5 countries made up 75% of world FDI outflows, as they have in earlier years.
†By assumption.

field. However, the use of GNP as the denominator incorporates a dimension of country size that was not included in the first measure. Just as smaller countries generally have larger ratios of exports to GNP, so one might expect the smaller European economies to exhibit higher ratios of FDI/GNP than those for the US or Japan. Indeed, the UK figure of 22% partly reflects both these factors: a small to medium-size economy with a long history of international investment. However, it should be remembered that ratios such as those in Table 2.4 have no intrinsic upper limits or *a priori* equilibrium levels. They are useful only in a comparative context over time or across countries.

Table 2.5 shows the basis of the quantification for outward FDI flows. Assumptions were chosen to be as simple and transparent as possible, and the result was checked for consistency with historical parameters such as those in Table 2.4. To avoid the problem of erratic annual figures, a three-year average (1986–8 inclusive) was taken as the base. FDI outflows were extrapolated in real terms at 5% per year for the US and UK, 15% per year for Japan and 10% per year for the other European countries and the rest of the world. Compared with developments over the last decade, these growth rates suggest a recovery in US outward flows (from 1% per annum), a slowdown in those from the UK (from 9% per annum), from Japan (from 17% per annum) and from France (from 12% per annum), and an acceleration for Germany (from 8% per annum) and the rest of the world. Thus, in the light of recent historical experience these assumed growth rates may appear conservative. However, they imply very large increases in the stock of FDI by 1995 and an almost explosive growth in the ratios from Table 2.4 for the UK and Japan. They also imply that EC companies take over the role that American companies played in the 1960s as the major international investors. In part this reflects new opportunities in Eastern Europe. By 1995 outward FDI from the EC as a whole (excluding intra-EC flows) reaches $65 billion, compared with outward US FDI of $38 billion and Japanese FDI of $60 billion (all in 1988 prices). If intra-EC flows are included, cross-border FDI by EC companies totals $90 billion in 1995.

Between 1988 and 1995 global FDI flows grow at an annual average rate of 9.2% in real terms, which is comfortably within the envelope of 6% to 15% derived from the elasticity estimates. The global *stock* of FDI is growing at over 12% per annum because the size of each increment (that is, the annual FDI flow) is so large relative to the stock in the base year (1988). This, in turn, is due to the very rapid growth in FDI over the last five years which, itself, has doubled the stock figures for Japan and increased those of the UK, France and Germany by more than 50% in real terms. Only the US stock of overseas assets was large enough relative to its annual outflows to have shown just a moderate increase (23% over the five years, or 4.2% per year). By the same token, if the quantification were extrapolated beyond 1995, stock growth rates from the 1995 base would settle down to moderate levels because the base itself would be so much higher.

This pattern of rapid expansion of the FDI stock induced by a moderate growth (in fact, a deceleration from recent trends) of FDI flows reflects the contention that we are in the middle of a decade (1985–95) when FDI gains its maturity as a major force for international economic integration. It is in this sense that quantitative increases in FDI flows have reached the threshold where they create a qualitatively different set of linkages among advanced economies.

3

GLOBAL COMPANIES AND NATIONAL ECONOMIES

The previous chapter documented the quickening of the pace of FDI flows during the 1980s and the emergence of the UK and Japan, in particular, as major international investors along with the United States. It suggested that this was caused partly by the favourable macroeconomic circumstances of the mid- to late 1980s, but that it was also given a powerful impetus by the opening up of service sectors to international competition and the emergence of Japan's external surplus. The impulse provided by these two developments will require five to ten years to run its course, and it is also expected to spread to smaller countries in the OECD area and beyond. An illustrative scenario for outward flows of FDI through the mid-1990s shows that the global stock in 1995 could well be more than double (2.2 times) the 1988 stock in real terms. This would happen if real FDI flows grow at an average annual rate of just over 9%, compared to their historical growth for the G-5 of 7% over the period 1980–8 and 19% over the five years since 1983.

What would such large increases in FDI mean from the point of view of the host economies? How important are foreign-owned firms in the macroeconomic aggregates of the advanced economies? How do the major countries compare in this respect? How are future flows likely to be distributed among host countries? Is the current flurry of concern in the US over the recent wave of inward FDI justified? In short, what are the benefits and costs of increased foreign penetration from the host country point of view? And, even if the benefits predominate, are there controls or safeguards that a country might employ to avoid or minimize the costs? Are such controls generalizable across countries or do they exhibit 'beggar thy neighbour' properties? To address such questions, this chapter considers the evidence from the Group of Five countries in the light of their comparative positions and policies towards inward FDI. It concludes with a scenario for the distribution of inward FDI flows through 1995 for the G-5 countries and the rest of the world.

At the global level, and over the long run, there is little doubt that increased FDI is a desirable component both of the *economic* adjustment process as countries grow and decline and of the international *political* adjustment needed to accommodate the decline in US hegemony, the growing economic weight of Japan and the greater political cohesiveness, and thus increased international influence, of Europe. It is nonetheless possible that particular countries – and certainly particular industries within countries – will lose from the economic integration process that greater FDI implies. It is natural that those who think they may lose will oppose an open policy towards FDI, notwithstanding its overall net benefits. Thus it is important to be clear about arguments which concern the size of the cake (i.e., economic efficiency and growth) and its distribution (particular winners and losers).

It is a standard finding in economics that trade-offs between efficiency and distribution can best be handled by maximizing efficiency and using some of the benefits generated to compensate the losers (for instance, through income and profits taxes). This works within a national context where transfers can be engineered through the political system. But there is no international mechanism for arranging such transfers. Thus, if it were the case that some *countries* would lose absolutely in an open FDI regime, they might wish to close their borders. Even then, however, the FDI would simply be diverted to other countries and the industries of the country closed to FDI would face increased competition from imports without the increased investment resources that FDI brings.

By analogy with trade theory, a presumption can be established that a country as a whole is unlikely to lose from open policies towards FDI. As discussed in the previous chapter, there are many possible motivations for a particular firm to engage in FDI, just as there are many possible motivations for it to trade. In either case, and for whatever reason, it believes that its profits could be increased by foreign-produced inputs and/or foreign sales. It is that 'first order' choice to enter foreign markets, either as a buyer or a seller (or both) which causes the dynamic of comparative advantage to operate, thereby ensuring that both countries benefit.

The 'second order' decision by the firm as to *how* it enters the foreign markets, as a trader or as an investor, is immaterial from the viewpoint of the eventual consumer who reaps the benefit of lower prices through the specialization and economies of scale that international integration makes possible. That consumer is purchasing mostly within his domestic market, which is coterminous with the political boundaries of his domicile. Thus, except for expatriates and purchases by travellers, the ultimate benefits from open markets (both for imports and for inward FDI) can still be defined in terms of the nation-state. They accrue to consumers and consumers have a clear domicile – unlike multinational companies. Thus the efficiency/distribution trade-off can still be considered in a national context. As discussed in Chapter 5, however, policies which are targeted to firms directly (such as tax incentives and industrial policy) can have pernicious welfare effects if there is a substantial presence of foreign-owned firms in an economy.

Inward investment: who is getting it and why?

As described in Chapter 1, the first wave of FDI in the postwar period was from the United States into Europe during the 1960s. In the 1970s, FDI spread more widely around the globe, largely in search of oil reserves. In the 1980s, British and Japanese firms expanded strongly overseas, mostly into the United States. German and French firms have been less active but more diversified in their targets, moving both into the US and into other European countries. It cannot yet be said that FDI flows have attained a structural maturity comparable to those of trade flows, where the links run in every direction and, in general, the largest exporters are also the largest importers. But we are starting to see more diversity of flows, a lessening of the dominant position of the US and even, except in the case of the Japanese, a relative balancing of inward/outward flows by country.

Table 3.1 summarizes the inward and outward flows of FDI for the G-5 countries during the 1980s. The US and the UK were the largest 'exporters' as well as 'importers' of FDI over this decade. The first column of the table highlights the large volume of FDI that has

Table 3.1 Inward and outward FDI in the G-5
(billion US $, total 1980–8)

	Inward	Outward
US	251.7	157.3
UK	64.7	133.2
Japan	2.9	96.0
Germany	9.1	52.5
France	27.9	43.3

gone into the US, the very small amount into Japan and the unusual ranking of the three European economies, with the smallest (Britain) attracting more than six times as much inward FDI as the largest (Germany). Germany is the only country of the G-5 where inward FDI flows were lower in the 1980s, in real terms, than in the 1970s.

The relative popularity of the US and UK as host countries for inward investment is consistent with the two factors cited in the section above as the dominant stimuli behind the 1980s FDI surge: services liberalization and the Japan factor. Both countries have been in the forefront of liberalization efforts and they have both received more than their proportional share of Japan's new FDI. Contrary to popular belief, it *cannot* be explained by the fall in the dollar since there were also large inward flows of FDI to the US when the dollar was at its peak in the mid-1980s.

The policy climate and composition of inward FDI for each of the G-5 countries is discussed later in this chapter. In addition to looking at FDI figures, however, it is instructive to compare the total importance of foreign-owned firms (FOFs) in the five economies. As shown in Figure 2.1 of the previous chapter, FOF measures include all firms with more than 10% foreign ownership regardless of whether the original investment was financed from foreign sources or domestically. Thus it is a broader measure than the balance-of-payments flows that constitute FDI. At the same time, FOF measures overstate the real importance of foreign-owned firms in an economy since there is clearly a qualitative difference between a firm which is 10% foreign-owned and one which is 90% foreign-owned. They are lumped together in the data and, as discussed in Chapter 4, this further compounds the problem of drawing implications about foreign *control* from figures of foreign *ownership*.

Table 3.2 Indices of FOF involvement in the G-5
(% of FOFs in total)

	US	Germany	UK	Japan	France
Sales	10[e]	19[b]	19[d]	1[a]	27[f]
Value added			17[d]		24[f]
Employment	4[a]	8[a]	13[d]	0.4[a]	20[f]
Assets	9[b]	17[b]	14[c]	1[a]	
Investment	8[b]		13[c]		19[f]
Exports	23	24	30	2	32
Imports	34			15	
Memo item:*					
Sales/imports	150	139	60	42	74

*Gross sales of goods by FOFs as a percentage of merchandise imports.
[a]All industries.
[b]All non-financial sectors.
[c]All large companies.
[d]Manufacturing.
[e]Manufacturing, wholesale, retail.
[f]Manufacturing, petroleum.

There are many measures of the macroeconomic importance of FOFs in an economy, none of which is theoretically superior for all purposes. In Europe, where the political debate revolves around employment, the most frequently cited statistic is the proportion of the labour force working for foreign-owned firms. In the US – an economy already at full employment – concerns relate more to the degree of foreign ownership of land and productive assets. In France, where the government has traditionally played an important role in planning and directing national investment, excellent data are available on the proportion of investment provided by FOFs, but not on the stock of assets owned by them. In Germany and Japan – where generating national investment resources is not a problem – data are not available on FOF investment although they do exist for FOF assets. Table 3.2 summarizes the available information across the five countries.

There is a striking difference between the level of FOF penetration in the European countries and that in the United States and Japan. Although the data coverage is not the same across countries (see the appendix for details), it is clear that FOFs are a much more important presence in the European countries than they are in the other two. Roughly one-fifth of domestic sales of manufactured goods and over one-quarter of exports in the three European countries of our sample (the E-3) are from foreign-owned firms. About 8% of total employment in Germany and 13–20% of manufacturing employment in the UK and France are with FOFs. They own around 15% of the asset base of the E-3.

In the United States, except for the foreign trade measures, the level of foreign-owned firm participation is roughly half that in the E-3 (about 10% of domestic sales or assets and 4% of employment). These are not insignificant amounts, but they are far from excessive by the standards of other advanced economies. On this basis, it is hard to understand the mounting concern about multinationals buying up America and taking over the industrial and technological base of the country (Tolchin and Tolchin, 1987). As noted below, such sentiment is more likely to be a reaction to the recent rapid *increase* in inward FDI than to its level, which remains low by international standards.

If the level of FOF involvement in the US economy can be described as low, then its level in Japan must be termed minuscule. Only 1% of domestic sales and 2% of Japanese exports are made by foreign-owned firms. They employ less than 1% of the labour force and own 1% of assets. Given these figures, it is surprising that FOFs account for 15% of Japan's imports. This high figure implies that most of the FOFs in Japan are distribution outlets – or even 'screwdriver' assembly plants – for their own imported products. The local content of the goods sold by FOFs in Japan is likely to be much lower than that of Japanese subsidiaries selling in the US or Europe!

One might advance three possible explanations for the large cross-country divergence in levels of FOF involvement. First, it may simply be a function of the size of the economy. The smaller European countries could be expected to have higher levels of FDI than the US, because intra-European investment would be included in their figures whereas a Massachusetts investment into California would not be counted in the US figures. Second, there could be policy differences toward FDI which have induced more into the E-3 than into the US or Japan. One often hears that developing countries need to adopt more liberal policies towards FOFs in order to attract more FDI. Third, it could simply be a matter of time. It was argued in the previous chapter that much of the increased *outward* flow of FDI during the 1980s represented a maturing of European and, especially, Japanese businesses which are now converging towards the American (and British) norm as active international investors. It could be that a similar convergence is under way on the side of inward investment – this time towards the European norm. To assess these three (not mutually exclusive) explanations requires a closer examination of the European, US and Japanese experiences as host countries.

The European countries: mature recipients
As shown in Table 3.2, the three European countries of the G-5 have roughly similar levels of foreign-owned firm participation in their economies. Yet Table 3.1 documented the much larger inflows of FDI that Britain has received over this decade compared to those of France and Germany. There are several possible explanations for this difference in the two measures. The most likely is timing. The largest inflows into the UK have occurred since 1986, while the FOF figures are drawn from a survey published in 1985. Even when these new investments have reached their production and employment capacity levels, the UK's FOF measures will change only slowly because they are drawn from the total stock of inward investment whereas FDI represents only the marginal flow. Since the big American FDI into Europe was in the 1960s, most of the FOF impact in all three countries relates to investments that originated in that era.

It is also possible that local borrowings are used for a greater proportion of foreign investment in Germany and France than in Britain. Because of the definitions of the two measures, this could result in smaller FDI into Germany than into Britain even with identical FOF involvement. But given the relative size of the two economies, and the fact that both have open capital markets, it is doubtful that financing methods could account for much of the difference.

Policy climate
The section above suggested three possible explanations for differing levels of inward FDI: the policy environment, the time pattern of

investment and the size of the economy. To begin with politics, the three countries have had quite different political attitudes towards FDI, at least until very recently. In France, until about 1985, inward FDI was positively discouraged both by the conservative government of Giscard d'Estaing and under the various incarnations of the Mitterrand presidency. This official attitude was reversed in 1985 by Prime Minister Chirac, but since many large industries were still in public hands, greenfield investments were the only channel open for major infusions of FDI. Under the privatization policies implemented subsequently, foreign interest in acquiring French companies has increased. However, the French government carefully limited foreign ownership in many of these to 20% (examples being Elf-Aquitaine, Saint-Gobain, Paribas) and retained the right to veto any unwanted bids.

With this discouraging policy stance, it is surprising that FOFs have attained such a high share of activity in the French economy. In part, it may be that in those manufacturing industries for which FDI has traditionally been important (oil, chemicals, automobiles), French firms are in a weak position compared to MNEs from the other four countries. Within the G-5, the oil industry is dominated by US and UK firms. In chemicals, the big firms are predominantly US and German; and for automobiles the largest MNEs are US, Japanese and German. Even in services, where Japan, the US and the UK all have strong international firms, the French firms have stayed in their own (until recently, heavily protected) market.

German policy towards inward FDI is ostensibly neutral, neither welcoming nor discouraging. In fact the heavily regulated federal system, the powerful German Cartel Office (which makes acquisitions difficult) and the extensive practice of co-determination, whereby workers have input at the board level, constitute solid obstacles to inward investment. In addition, the regional (*Länder*) governments are active sponsors of local firms, and buy-outs are made difficult by the position of German banks as large shareholders and loyal supporters of existing management. These are all factors which apply equally to German firms wishing to expand domestically via takeover, so it cannot be said that government policy discriminates against FOFs. But for a foreign firm comparing Germany with other possible investment locations in the European market, they are obstacles nonetheless.

In addition, in the service sectors, Germany lags behind the UK and France in privatizing and liberalizing service providers. Attempts to lower the government's involvement in Lufthansa were blocked by domestic opposition. There is little sign that the Bundespost will follow the example of British Telecom in being privatized. The financial sector is free of capital controls, but numerous practices remain which effectively curtail foreign participation in insurance and retail banking. Of course, there are also purely economic factors, such as high labour costs and a strong currency, which for some industries make Germany a less attractive site than other parts of the European Community such as the UK or Spain.

Given these factors, it is perhaps not surprising that FDI inflows into Germany have been lower in the 1980s, in real terms, than they were in the latter half of the 1970s – unlike the other four countries studied. How can this fact be reconciled with the high levels of FOF involvement in the German economy? It is mainly a matter of timing. As discussed below, FOFs have been important to the German economy since the 1960s; their level of participation has not increased in recent years.

By contrast with the situation in Germany and France, British policy towards FDI has been a welcoming one since the Thatcher government came to power in 1979. It established a liberal policy towards both inward and outward FDI. It quickly released UK-based MNEs from the burden of exchange controls, and it has shown its willingness to protect the interests of foreign MNEs located in Britain. In the case of automobile exports to France from the UK-based Nissan plant, the EC Commission eventually upheld the British government's position – against a complaint brought by the French – that local content levels between 60% and 65% were sufficient for the cars to be considered British-made.

There have been occasional lapses in the general welcome given to inward investment in Britain, which illustrate the kinds of political concerns that FDI can arouse even in a liberal environment. The Westland helicopter case in 1986 caused the resignation of two government ministers. The issue was partly whether the company should be sold to a European or an American bidder. The government sided with Westland's board which favoured the US offer, but it was criticized for not seeking an alliance with other European companies. In that case conflict was created by the nationality of the competitive bidders, and not by the question of whether a foreign takeover should be allowed at all.

49

In 1988 a Swiss company made an unwelcome bid for Rowntree, a British food conglomerate with many popular brandnames in the chocolate and sweets markets. The government declined to refer the bid to the Monopolies and Mergers Commission, since it did not consider that a merger would create a dominant market position. There was much criticism from UK companies, however, of the fact that the Swiss firm was itself immune from takeover because of the structure of its shareholding and its position under Swiss legislation. Calls for a 'level playing field' to equalize the positions of British and other European companies in takeover battles are sure to be heard whenever hostile offers come from immune firms. This is one of the most difficult policy issues discussed in Chapter 5.

With regard to subsidies for inward investment, the UK has not been particularly generous. Its policy has been to match what others offer to the extent possible, but also to ensure that the same incentives are available for domestic firms willing to locate or expand in the favoured region. Most FDI into Britain – including all of that into service industries – has come with no subsidy or tax incentive attached.

There are, however, also structural and more deep-seated reasons for the large volume of FDI flows into Britain. On the structural side, the UK has proceeded further than any country other than the US in the deregulation and liberalization of its financial and certain other service markets. The privatization of large industries such as British Petroleum, British Airways and British Telecom created new opportunities for foreign shareholdings, as well as domestic. (However, in the case of British Petroleum, a large purchase by the Kuwait Investment Office was referred to the Monopolies Commission and the purchaser was forced to divest itself of part of its shareholding.) The cultural ties, legal traditions and linguistic affinity between Britain and the United States must also account for a part of the long-standing preference of US MNEs for British-based European operations. Thirty-five percent of the total US FDI into the EC has gone into Britain. Because the US has been the largest overseas investor for so many years, the preference of American firms for Britain as an overseas location has naturally bulked up Britain's total inward FDI.

Now it appears that the same phenomenon is at work with the Japanese. Although the largest single share of their FDI has gone to the US, the UK has been by far the favoured location in the EC.

Table 3.3 Distribution of Japanese and US firms in the EC* (percentage shares of total in EC)

	United States		Japan	
	FDI	Employment	FDI	Employment
UK	38	33	38	30
Germany	17	23	8	15
Netherlands	12	5	20	3
Luxembourg	1		17	2†
France	10	15	6	15
Italy	7	8	1	3
Spain	3	7	4	22

Sources: US Commerce Department; Ministry of Finance; JETRO.
*US FDI: Position, 1988.
 US Employment: Nonbank affiliates, 1987
 Japanese FDI: Cumulative total, 31 March 1989.
 Japanese Employment: Manufacturing, 1988, all Europe.
†Belgium and Luxembourg.

Table 3.3 depicts the share of US and Japanese FDI in each of the major European countries as a percentage of their total FDI in the European Community. The share of each country in the total employment of US- and Japanese-owned firms in the EC is added for comparison.

The preference of Japanese firms for the UK is a relatively new development, unlike the long-standing US involvement in Britain. Table 3.4 shows the pattern of establishments of Japanese manufacturing firms in the EC over time. Whereas Germany was the prime location in the 1970s, the scale has tipped heavily in favour of the UK since 1980, with 63 new establishments – twice the number of France or Germany. Spain has also become an important location for labour-intensive production by Japanese companies since it joined the EC. This newly revealed preference of Japanese firms for the UK is a reflection of the improvement in the UK's economic prospects during the 1980s, the liberalization of its domestic regulations in the banking field and the more positive government attitude towards Japan that has been slowly emerging.

The preference of US and Japanese investors for one EC member over another cannot be ascribed to any one cause. There is a

Table 3.4 Japanese manufacturing investment in Europe
(number of establishments per time period)

	Before 1971	1972–9	1980–7	1987–8
UK	4	14	50	13
France	7	5	26	1
Germany	7	19	26	6
Spain	5	9	18	4
Total Europe	36	80	162	33

Source: 'Current Management Situation of Japanese Manufacturing Enterprises in Europe', JETRO 1988.

complex mix of economic, political, cultural and legal factors influencing investment decisions. There is still considerable divergence of legislation in the major European countries regarding foreign investment. In some areas, notably competition policy, the EC agreed in 1990 to create a 'one-stop' clearing house, which will apply to bids over a certain minimum size by both EC and non-EC firms. This will probably stimulate total flows, but it is difficult to predict whether it will lead to a more or a less even dispersion of FDI across the EC. For this reason, the 1995 scenario for inward investment, developed at the end of this chapter, treats the EC as a single unit.

The general conclusion of this review of FDI policies in the E-3 is that differing attitudes towards inward FDI seem to have affected recent flows but have not yet resulted in commensurate differences in FOF participation in the three economies. These differences may show up in the future, as the variations in FDI inflows gradually make their mark on the FOF measures through increases in areas such as domestic production. However, it is worth considering other possible explanations for the large presence of FOFs in the E-3 economies compared with the US and Japanese levels.

Convergence over time
An historical perspective is provided in Table 3.5, which summarizes the FOF situation in the three countries currently (or at least as recently as data permit) and approximately a decade ago. We have seen that over this period FDI inflows increased both in the UK and France although they stagnated in Germany. We have also seen that

Table 3.5 FOF involvement in the E-3 (%)

	UK		France		Germany	
Manufacturing sector	1977	1986	1977	1986	1977	1986
Sales	22	19	24	26	17*	18*
Employment	15	13	18	21	14	13
Investment	21	22	19	19	NA	NA

*All non-financial corporate businesses.

much of the recent FDI has been in the service sectors, so it is particularly unfortunate that the E-3 data for FOFs cover only manufacturing. On this partial measure the FOF measures, for all three countries, show very little change. Levels of FOF participation in E-3 manufacturing were as high in 1977 as they are today. Foreign-owned firms have grown at roughly the same pace as the rest of the economy. The build-up of their participation levels in Europe occurred prior to the last decade. One might even hypothesize that a type of equilibrium level – in the manufacturing sector – has been reached in these economies and then maintained over the last decade. Similar participation levels may be approached over the next few years in the service sectors. It is possible that even higher levels will be reached, since trade in many services is not a viable alternative to investment.

Economic size
The final aspect to be considered for the E-3 is the ownership pattern of their FOFs. Do these high levels of foreign participation derive from the small size of the countries themselves? This can be answered in part by separating out the portion of FOF measures that derives from companies originating in other EC countries. While strictly comparable figures are not available for the three countries, approximately 30–40% of their inward FDI stock has come from other countries of the EC, while the US has accounted for 40–50%. Japan's share is only 1–2%. Thus if the EC countries were to be considered as a unit, for purposes of comparison with the US economy, the shares of FOF participation in the E-3 would fall to the 12–14% range rather than 20%. This is still higher than that

of the US, but not by a factor of two as before.* Thus, of the three explanations considered for differing levels of FOF participation, the most powerful seems to be convergence of patterns over time.

The United States: suddenly deluged

The counterpart of the surge in outward FDI flows of the 1980s has been the flood of inward investment into the United States. Although the US has been the world's largest foreign direct investor for decades, it attracted very little inward investment from the end of World War I until the end of the 1970s. This was probably due to the relative immaturity and domestic orientation of foreign firms rather than to any lack of market opportunities in the US or to its policy stance towards inward investment, which has long been an open one. It may also reflect the erosion of the technological and managerial superiority with which US industry emerged from World War II, which made it an effective competitor abroad and, even more so, in its home market (Graham and Krugman, 1989).

In 1979–80 this situation began to change radically. A step change in the size of inflows occurred, from an average of $7 billion/year in the three-year period prior to that shift to an average of $15 billion/ year (both in 1980 prices) in the three-year period following the shift. Whereas in 1977 the total stock of inward investment in the United States was smaller than that in Canada and only slightly larger than that in the UK or Germany, by 1985 it was over twice as large as in Canada and three to four times as large as in the UK or Germany. Another ramification of this shift has been a whittling away of the US *net* FDI position. Whereas in 1980 the stock of US FDI overseas was more than three times as large as foreign FDI in the US, by 1987 it was only 19% larger.† In 1988, for the first time since World War I, the recorded cumulative value of foreign direct investments in the US exceeded total US direct investment abroad.

The countries most responsible for the inward flood of FDI are Britain and Japan. The value of their FDI into the US has grown at

---

*The adjustment made for the E-3 by separating out intra E-3 flows does not fully take account of differences in country size since the aggregate GNP of the three countries is still only about half that of the US (in purchasing power parity terms).
†The outward stock is understated relative to the inward stock because both are recorded at book value, while outward FDI is generally older and therefore valued in less inflated dollars. In addition, if adjustment is made for Netherlands Antilles finance affiliates, the outward stock is 23% higher than the inward one.

the astonishing annual average rates of 28% and 35%, respectively, between 1980 and 1989. It has thus risen from 18% to 31% of the stock of FDI in the US for Britain and from 6% to 16% for Japan. These rising shares have been mostly at the expense of Canadian companies, whose share of foreign-owned assets in the United States has shrunk from 15% in 1980 to 8% in 1988, although in absolute terms Canadian FDI in the US has grown by $15 billion ($7 billion in 1980 prices) over this period. The German and French shares of US inward FDI have fallen slightly from 9% to 7% and from 4% to 3% respectively.

Measured by investment sector, services are now the largest, accounting for 49% of the total stock of inward FDI by the end of 1988. The share represented by petroleum has fallen, from 15% in 1980 to 11% in 1988, and manufacturing's share has fallen from 40% to 37% over the same period. Nonetheless, in some manufacturing subsectors there has been significant FDI and the share of the domestic production accounted for by foreign-owned firms has greatly increased. In motor vehicles and equipment, for example, where there has been heavy Japanese investment, the FDI position has almost doubled over the five-year period 1984–8.

In the United States policies towards inward investment are neutral in concept and as welcoming in fact as those of the UK. Subsidies are not offered at the federal level, but many states compete with each other to provide tax holidays and free sites to attract large new investors.

The effect of the increased FDI into the United States on measures of FOF importance is shown in Table 3.6. In contrast to the static situation in the European countries, most such measures have doubled in the last decade for the United States. Nonetheless, the levels of FOF participation in the US are still far below those in the E-3. A comparison is probably best centred on the figures for manufacturing employment, since investment figures are unavailable for Germany and sales figures in the US case look unnaturally high (compared with other US measures), probably because they include sales from foreign-owned distribution companies which are not actually manufacturing in the US. The average FOF share of manufacturing employment in the E-3 is 16%. If we reduce this by 35% to account for the intra-EC 'regional' flows, a comparable figure for the US would be 10%, to be set against its actual figure of 7%. Thus, even with the recent growth of FOF participation in the

Table 3.6 FOF involvement in the US economy (%)

	1977	1986
Gross sales	5	10
Total employment	2	4
Manufacturing employment	3	7
Total assets	5	9
Manufacturing assets	4	9
Total investment	4	8
Manufacturing investment	3	7

US economy, its current levels would have to increase by about 40% to reach comparable European figures.

However, public concern in the US about FOFs is clearly growing and a provision was included in the 1988 Omnibus Trade Act (the Exon-Floria Amendment) empowering the president to block foreign takeovers on national security grounds. Under the procedures established, this would only happen after a case was considered by a high-level intergovernmental committee which would make a recommendation (if unanimous) or send a statement of opposing views (if not) to the president. He would then decide whether to block the transaction, taking into consideration whether there was reason to believe that the foreign firm might take action that would impair the national security. This is a fairly tightly drawn statute, with time limits for reviews and decisions, but its real test will be through the history of its implementation. So far, of the more than 100 voluntary notifications that the committee has received, only two have been sent to President Bush with a statement of opposing views and he has let both go ahead (one after a restructuring of its takeover offer to exclude production related to nuclear weapons).

There is also a bill before Congress (originally called the Bryant Amendment) to impose stricter reporting requirements on foreign firms operating in the United States. Such firms are already obliged to disclose information to the Commerce Department, which publishes periodic tables and analyses of the aggregate data. However, firm-specific information is kept confidential and is not available even to members of Congress or to the President. The original version of the Bryant Amendment would have required open disclosure of this firm-specific – and thus potentially commercially sensitive – information. The disclosure provision has been dropped, but even the modified version of the Amendment, if it is enacted, would be a departure from the general US policy of neutrality (national treatment) towards foreign firms because it would impose reporting requirements on them which are not required of domestic firms (Graham and Krugman, 1989). It is for this reason that so much attention, both nationally and internationally, has been given to a relatively insignificant legislative proposal as it winds its tortuous way through the US legislative process.

Japan: Tokugawa revisited?

Until the early 1980s, the Japanese government maintained a policy of suspicion towards both outward and inward FDI. Before making an overseas investment, Japanese companies had to have approval from the Ministry of Finance. Inward FDI was only welcome if it provided greater access to raw materials or to foreign technology. Faced with foreign pressure, as well as a dramatic turnaround in its balance-of-payments position, Japan relaxed this regulation in 1980 so that notification alone is required for outward FDI. In 1984 MITI created an Office for the Promotion of Foreign Investment in Japan. The export promotion agency, JETRO, has also been reorganized to help attract inward investment and the Japan Development Bank now offers financing for inward investors as well as for Japanese companies.

By nationality of ownership, the US dominates inward investment in Japan, just as it does in the other four countries. Although only 4% of US outward FDI goes to Japan, US companies in Japan account for nearly half of the cumulative inward investment that has taken place since the statistical series began in 1951.

The major remaining barrier to inward investment is the Japanese business culture itself. Hostile takeovers are almost unthinkable, whether by domestic or foreign firms, and, in any case the cross-holdings of shares among companies and their lead banks effectively preclude such takeovers. Western business practices such as competitive tendering are much less common in Japan, so that new

Table 3.7 FOF involvement in Japan (%)

	1977	1986
Gross sales	2	1
Total employment	1	0.4
Manufacturing employment	2	1
Total assets	2	1
Manufacturing assets	5	2

businesses have trouble winning contracts even if their prices are competitive (Prestowitz, 1988). Of course, this is equally a problem for new Japanese companies. Thus it is consistent with the notion of neutrality towards or national treatment of FOFs, as recommended by the OECD and as applied in the US and many European countries.

Nonetheless, the system must be examined in operation. As shown in Table 3.7, not only is the share of FOFs in Japan's economic aggregates very low, but it has actually *decreased* over the last decade. The economy as a whole has grown rapidly over this period, so such a decrease in the FOF share does not imply that foreign firms have been pulling investment out of Japan. In fact, Japan's balance-of-payments data show that in real terms, average annual inflows during 1980–8 was 30% greater than the 1970s average. But this growth has taken place from a very small base and within the context of a rapidly growing domestic economy. Although the Japanese economy today is nearly half the size of the US economy, the stock of inward FDI in the US is between 40 and 60 times (depending on which measure is used) as large as inward FDI in Japan.

How much, if at all, is this situation likely to change? By industry, most FOF participation is still in the energy- and resource-intensive sectors: oil, rubber, chemicals and nonferrous metals. These provide at least some grounds for believing that there is scope for increased foreign market share once the FOFs become 'insiders' in the Japanese system: in the oil and coal industries, over one-third of total sales in Japan are by FOFs. Of course, in many other countries without oil or coal resources of their own, FOFs account for even larger proportions of the market in those sectors. Nonetheless, the current shares of FOFs are so low by the standards of other advanced economies that increases are likely, although they will probably be gradual because of the structural nature of the obstacles facing FOFs.

There are two areas in which the change is likely to be more rapid. Liberalization of the Japanese financial markets has led to an influx of foreign banks and securities houses, especially US and British ones. There is continued pressure for further market opening, and it is clear from the large profits of Japanese financial institutions that the market is not yet saturated. The other area where the market for new investment from overseas is opening up is in the sectors that have been partially or fully privatized. These include telecommunications (NTT), airlines (a partial sale of JAL), railways (JR) and other sectors such as tobacco.

Japanese companies have been highly successful in a number of high-technology export markets. Their international competitiveness is honed in a domestic market where consumers set high standards and where domestic companies compete fiercely (Turner, 1987; Harvey-Jones, 1988). For an FOF to succeed in that market is thus particularly difficult. A parallel may be drawn with the dominant market position held by American companies in the 1950s and 1960s. During that period, US firms were heavy international investors (mainly in Europe) while very few foreign firms were able to compete successfully in the US home market. It took nearly 15 years from the time when the US became an important source of outward FDI (1965) until it began to receive large inward flows (1979). If we date Japan's emergence as a major international investor from 1981, and if the US pattern is an appropriate guide, then we may expect strong inflows into Japan to begin in the latter half of the 1990s. In fact, the competitive pressures in a growing range of industries that now function in a global market-place, coupled with the strong interest of MNEs in the rapidly growing East Asian region, will probably hasten this trend.

Costs and benefits of inward investment

This chapter began with a set of questions, some of which required factual answers about the importance of FOFs in these five countries and how they compare both across countries and over time; and some of which required more speculative analysis about the potential benefits and possible costs to the host country of growing FOF participation. We can now turn to this second set of questions.

Conventional benefits and externalities

The potential benefits to a host country from increased FDI can be divided into two types: the conventional gains from economic integration and the externalities that may result from FDI over and above the strictly economic benefits that motivated firms to undertake the investment in the first place (Graham and Krugman, 1989). The first kind of gains are exactly the same as those attributed to the opening of markets through trade. The three most often cited are comparative advantage (i.e., the gains from specialization across larger areas), increasing returns (i.e., the ability to reach optimal production/organization size by selling into a larger market) and increased competition (i.e., reducing monopoly power and lowering prices to consumers by subjecting more firms to competition from the most efficient ones in their industry). It should not be surprising that FDI would lead to the same kinds of benefits as trade, because its motivation at the firm level is often identical.

The second kind of gain arising from inward FDI concerns the spin-offs that may accrue to other (domestic) firms in the economy from the introduction by the foreign firm of superior technology or management methods. These spin-offs occur both through the demonstration effect and through the mobility of labour between foreign and domestic firms. The basic idea is that the foreign firm which succeeds in the domestic market because of some ownership advantage that it possesses is not able fully to capture the benefits from that advantage. Many LDCs claim to value these external gains from FDI (including the training of local workers) more highly than the direct economic benefits, such as increased exports, that it brings.

There is some evidence in the UK that British firms are adopting Japanese-style management techniques and that such rethinking of management behaviour is responsible for some of the impressive productivity gains that have been recorded since the mid-1980s. A recent survey of 64 British-owned manufacturing firms found that over 90% of respondents were using, or planning to use, 'Japanese' techniques such as team working (as distinct from traditional assembly-line production), multi-skilling, subcontracting and total quality control. Moreover, most firms that had tried such practices said that they had been successful (Oliver and Wilkinson, 1988).

Unfortunately, it is not possible in any satisfactory way to quantify either the direct or the indirect benefits from FDI. Here again, there is a similarity with trade. One of the major obstacles economists face in arguing the case for free trade is that it is relatively easy to measure the immediate costs that accrue to a particular firm or set of workers who are displaced by foreign competitors, whereas it is generally impossible to measure the much more widespread and dynamic benefits that displacement brings to the economy as a whole (Henderson, 1986).

This situation is not helped by those advocates of FDI who commit the same fallacy by claiming that a particular inward investment will create x hundred new jobs. Although the new plant may well employ a workforce of that size, many of the new workers hired will come from the ranks of the already employed. The worker has a new job, but the economy may not. At the margin there may be some fall in economy-wide unemployment, but the linkage is far from one-to-one. In the extreme case of an economy already at full employment (such as the US and many regions in Europe today), the direct employment effect will be to bid up wages. In addition, new jobs in one plant may well be at the expense of lost jobs in another, if the new competitor (whether domestic or foreign) is indeed more efficient and captures market share from established firms. The undue and often misplaced focus in the public debate on the employment effects of FDI is an obstacle to developing a more appropriate policy stance.

For developing countries which are capital constrained, FDI can bring large incremental benefits since it is likely to be an addition to, rather than a substitute for, domestic investment; and it creates similar multiplier effects on the rest of the economy. But in advanced economies where firms are able to borrow or raise new equity on international capital markets, it is difficult to claim that new FDI represents net incremental investment. This is especially true for foreign takeovers of existing firms. Yet the same microeconomic benefits (gains from specialization, increasing returns to scale and more competition) flow from takeovers as from greenfield investment. The distinction often drawn in the public debate between 'good' employment-generating greenfield investment and 'bad' foreign takeovers is a spurious one.

61

What are the perceived costs or possible problems created by inward FDI? Here it is useful to distinguish among four categories, two of which parallel the two benefit cases described above: non-economic costs, direct economic costs, external economic costs and concerns relating to reciprocity of market access.

Non-economic costs

The first category, non-economic concerns, generally relate either to national security or the preservation of cultural values. In the UK both of these areas are covered by the 'public interest' criterion which the Department of Trade and Industry is entitled to apply to assess the acceptability of takeovers. Indeed, few countries would allow foreign takeovers of their key defence contractors. In the US there was felt to be a need to give the president explicit authority in such cases, which is why the Exon-Floria Amendment was included in the 1988 Omnibus Trade Bill. In addition, the US restricts foreign ownership of domestic air transport, nuclear energy production and most domestic maritime transport.

One of the contentious aspects of the new competition policy directives being drafted in the European Commission concerns the extent to which member states should be allowed a 'backstop' or second-level veto on takeovers which clear the EC's tests for preserving competition in the European market. If second-level vetoes are permitted, the grounds for them should be clearly specified and would probably include national security and cultural preservation. The main example of the latter is the limits which many countries place on the ownership of broadcasting stations. In the US a special waiver is required before FOFs can purchase more than 20% of a company with a broadcasting licence. In Europe, many of the major broadcasting companies are still publicly owned, but if they are privatized it is unlikely that unlimited foreign purchase will be allowed.

Direct economic costs

Second, there are concerns about the direct economic effects of FDI in sectors which exhibit market imperfections of various types. Here there are two main arguments, both of which parallel those used in the trade policy literature. The more straightforward argument concerns the need to avoid 'unfair' competition caused by the entry into the domestic market of foreign firms which receive direct or indirect subsidies from their government. In the field of trade, such cases are dealt with in the anti-dumping and anti-subsidy clauses in the GATT. The EC has made explicit the link between 'unfair' trade and FDI by extending its right to impose dumping duties on goods produced by foreign firms in the Community if their investment took place after an anti-dumping complaint was filed. Unfortunately, the EC's anti-dumping machinery and the way it is used violate so many economic principles that such a link merely extends an already flawed policy into areas where its eventual costs to the EC may be even greater (Davenport, 1989). The general applicability of anti-subsidy and anti-dumping policies to FDI is discussed in Chapter 5.

The second direct economic concern about inward investment parallels the case made in the strategic trade literature. The basic argument is that in some industries size is so important, perhaps because of increasing returns to scale (such as the need to spread R&D expenditures across large production runs), that it is an effective entry barrier against new competitors. In that case, the only way for a country to develop domestic firms which could compete in such markets is to keep out foreign competition until the domestic firms have reached the necessary size.

It is a fairly standard mathematical exercise to derive an appropriate tariff for such cases, given a full set of assumptions about the degree of scale economies in the industry, the elasticity of consumer demand, etc. (see, e.g., Krugman and Obstfeld, 1988). But to turn this mathematical result into a solid policy recommendation presents two large problems. First, the necessary data both on supply (production functions) and demand (elasticities) are impossible to obtain for most industries. If the experience of the postwar period has taught us anything, it is that the microeconomy is a dynamic creature; technology is changing, consumer preferences change, Schumpeter's process of creative destruction is a widespread one across industries. Even if one could estimate the necessary parameters from historical data, to extrapolate them into the future would require an unacceptable leap of logic.

Assuming for the moment, however, that this first problem of data could somehow be overcome, the second problem that a strategically trading government may face is that its partners decide to retaliate by imposing their own tariffs (or barriers) against its goods (or investment). Then we are into the realm of game theory and all bets are off as to who benefits; in the general case, both countries lose relative to the no-tariff (no-barrier) case.

Before dismissing the strategic case for investment barriers on the practical and political grounds discussed above, it is perhaps worth asking how large a segment of the typical modern economy is likely to be subject to economies of scale so extreme that they constitute entry barriers and thus provide scope for competitive exploitation by FOFs. The answer clearly depends on the size of the economy. For the Netherlands, for example, there must be many industries for which the domestic market is insufficient to grow fully competitive firms.* For the European Community as a whole, however, there are probably few such cases. The example which recurs again and again in the trade literature is aerospace (Airbus versus Boeing). Beyond that, the general pattern has been that 'new' industries, such as computers and telecommunications, tend to arouse fears of monopoly domination in their early days (when they have new patents to exploit and the market is still small) which are proved false as the market grows, competitors spring up and the industry matures. Neither technological advances nor consumer preferences have shown a general tendency to increase scale economies. The case of IBM is a familiar example of this phenomenon of initial market concentration followed by dispersion and increased competition as demand develops.

Finally, however, suppose that a particular government believed that its economy was vulnerable to abuse from global companies which, if allowed to set up facilities in the local market, would drive all of the domestic competitors out of business. The question would still remain whether a restrictive policy towards FDI would be the best instrument to use to avoid such abuse without unwanted costs in other areas. The answer must be that an effective competition policy would be a better approach, since it could be targeted on those FOFs which might pose a threat to competitive markets while allowing other FDI to proceed unhindered.

External economic costs
The third general concern with inward FDI is that it might have

---

*Note that even for the small country case, the presumption that the best approach to such a market failure is to restrict trade and investment has not been established. The Netherlands is an example of a country which has benefited greatly from an open-door policy toward trade and FOFs, enabling it to develop its own fully competitive global companies by deliberately exposing them to open competition from the beginning in the home market. Hong Kong has demonstrated the success of an even more extreme version of the same philosophy.

external costs to the rest of the economy because FOFs may create fewer spin-offs to other economic sectors than do domestic firms. This argument is analogous to the case for external benefits from FDI discussed above. Basically it hinges on the supposition that foreign firms, as a group, may behave differently from domestic firms, as a group. This may bring benefits, as when those differences relate to superior technology and management practices. However, it may also bring costs. For example, when an American firm takes over a Scottish company, that company's financial dealings may be shifted from the Bank of Scotland to the Bank of America. When a downturn develops in a global industry, a foreign headquarters may lay off workers at its overseas plants more quickly than would a domestic firm in the same industry.

As was the case with external benefits, the size – and even the probability – of these external costs is very difficult to assess. Presumably the American firm was able to offer a higher price to the shareholders of the Scottish firm because it saw a way to increase the firm's profitability. Increased profitability often brings expansion, which would produce offsetting gains to the local economy. Moreover, those shareholders who sold out now have more capital to invest in other local industries if they so choose. With respect to lay-offs and plant closures, there is some evidence to suggest that FOFs are *less* likely than domestic firms to leave a market in response to a downturn because they have incurred higher costs in getting into the market in the first place. If they perceive that the downturn may be temporary, they have a higher threshold of 'avoidance costs' to overcome before it is wise to pull out and face the risk of having to go back into the market later (Krugman, 1988). An OECD study on structural adjustment and MNEs concluded that

the strategies and reactions of multinational and domestic enterprises to structural change have been generally parallel... For instance, ... multinational enterprises do not resort more to the closure of an entity, in comparison to their domestic counterparts ... their employment performance has been equal to, and in some cases superior to, domestic firms.' (OECD, *Structural Adjustment and Multinational Enterprises*, Paris, 1985)

It is also difficult to generalize about the relative productivity of foreign-owned and domestic firms. Comparisons based on aggregate data can be misleading because FOF investment from particular countries is often concentrated in particular sectors rather than spread in a representative way over the entire economy. For example, aggregate data for the UK show that the labour productivity (gross value added per employee) of Italian-owned manufacturing firms is 2.3 times the British average while that of Japanese-owned manufacturing firms in the UK is only about 70% of the national average. However, the Italian figures are likely to come from a very small sample of investment in a high-priced goods sector, while case study evidence suggests that workers in Japanese-owned plants often achieve major advances in productivity over those in British-owned firms in the same highly competitive, and thus low-margin, sectors (Dunning, 1985).

There have also been studies of the extent to which global companies tend to keep research and other 'high spin-off value' activities at headquarters. In a large empirical study covering both US and European multinationals, little evidence was found of any 'headquarters effect' except in companies that have become multinational only recently (Cantwell, 1989, as cited in Graham and Krugman, 1989). Certainly the widespread R&D activities of IBM, Hewlett-Packard and ICI seem to add support to this view. Thus the working assumption for the policy analyst must be that FOFs do not systematically behave in a different way from domestic firms.

Differential market access
A final area of public concern relating to FDI, at least in the US and the UK, is the differing degrees of openness towards inward investment, especially via takeovers, that characterize various countries. The very small penetration of FOFs into Japan and the decline in real inward investment in Germany during a period when all the other G-5 countries were showing rapid increases was noted above. Again, this worry is comparable to that in trade policy, where an international system of negotiating reciprocal reductions in barriers (the GATT) was needed to achieve the benefits that economists had repeatedly demonstrated would flow from unilateral reductions. To extend the discussion above about 'strategic' investment policy, if there are large-scale economies in an industry such as banking (where most international competition is via investment rather than trade), and if one country's market is open to inward investment

while a second country's is not, then the banks from the second country will gain a strategic advantage from operating in both markets which is denied to the banks from the first country.

This is probably the single most important and most difficult policy issue related to inward investment. A negotiating approach to achieve the long-term objective of a level playing field for FDI is outlined in Chapter 5. In the meantime, a small start is being made through the negotiations in the current GATT Round on trade-related investment measures (TRIMs). Because FDI flows are so heavily concentrated among the OECD countries, however, of greater immediate significance are the bilateral and regional arrangements that are emerging. The US-Canada Free Trade Agreement clears many of the regulatory obstacles to the establishment of FOFs in the service sectors of both economies. The EC's Second Banking Directive incorporates reciprocity of access provisions designed to open markets for European banks, particularly in Japan. Negotiations between the EC and EFTA countries may also produce an accord on takeover codes and rights of establishment for foreign-owned firms.

The 1990s: patterns of penetration

At the end of the previous chapter a sample quantification was developed for outward investment flows up to the end of 1995 based on certain assumptions. That scenario can now be extended to inward flows, recognizing that for the world as a whole, outward and inward flows must balance.

The three underlying assumptions discussed in Chapter 2 are still relevant. FDI is treated as a global phenomenon which, like trade, tends to intensify among countries as the range of opportunities expands into new sectors. It is not viewed primarily as a transfer of capital from low-return countries to high-return ones. The international economic and political climate are extrapolations of the recent past; i.e., no major economic recessions or serious intensification of political friction among the OECD countries is assumed. In other words, the political/economic background is business as usual.

Individual country projections were developed using the overall constraint that outward and inward flows must balance and taking account of the historical and comparative positions of each country or region. The EC is treated as a whole because of the difficulty noted above of guessing whether an internal market without barriers will tend to concentrate or disperse the increased total inflows that are expected.

For the largest recipient country, the United States, it is assumed that the growth of inward FDI slows from the 7.2% average annual rate of the 1980s to 6% per year (in real terms) during 1988–95. This is still a higher rate than the US experienced in earlier decades, but reflects a shift in the focus of global FDI flows from the US to Europe. The renewed attraction of Europe is, of course, the economic growth through market integration that the 1992 process is expected to provoke. Thus the share of global FDI going to the EC is assumed to rise from an estimated 21.3% in 1986–8 to 25% in the 1988–95 period. This implies an average annual growth rate of 11.7% in real FDI flows into the EC over this period. Finally, FDI inflows into Japan are assumed to grow tenfold between 1988 and 1995. This would raise them from their very low current level to a figure midway between *current* flows into France and Germany. This assumption is probably as optimistic as one could reasonably make, yet FDI into the world's second largest economy would still represent less than 2% of global flows by 1995. These assumptions and their implications for other figures in the scenario are set out in Table 3.8, where ROWE represents the rest of the world excluding the countries of the EC, the US and Japan.

In this quantification the US and the EC receive about the same size of FDI inflows. The rest of the world – which includes the EFTA countries, Eastern Europe, Canada, Australia, and the newly industrializing countries of East Asia as well as the developing world – receive a slightly larger share of the rapidly growing pie. Some progress is made towards a more widespread and even distribution of flows, although Japan's exceptional position changes very little. As a host country, it is not expected to blossom until the latter half of the 1990s.

The full matrix of inward and outward flows is shown in Table 3.9. The horizontal and vertical totals are from Tables 2.9 and 3.8. The distribution of totals within cells is purely notional, based on historical patterns for each country. Figures in the diagonal cells for the EC and ROWE represent cross-country investment within the category; e.g., German investment in France or Austrian investment in Hungary.

Table 3.8 Inward FDI flows in 1995
(billion 1988 US $)

	Av. ann. FDI inflow 1986–8	Composition of inflows 1986–8 %	FDI inflows 1995	Composition of inflows 1995 %	Av. ann. growth 1988–95 %
US	39.4	31.9	59.2	25.9	6.0†
EC	26.3*	21.3	57.2	25.0†	11.7
Japan	0.3	0.2	3.0	1.3	38.9
ROWE	57.4*	46.5	109.4	47.8	9.7
Total	123.4	100	228.8‡	100	9.2

*Estimate based on assumption that 65% of EC inflows went to the UK, France and Germany, as they did in earlier years.
†By assumption.   ‡From Table 2.5.

Table 3.9 1995 matrix of FDI flows
(billion 1988 US $)

To \ From	US	EC	Japan	ROWE	Inward total
US	–	40.0	15.0	4.2	59.2
EC	13.0	25.0	14.0	5.2	57.2
Japan	1.5	0.8	–	0.7	3.0
ROWE	23.8	24.2	31.4	30.0	109.4
Outward total	38.3	90.0	60.4	40.1	228.8

The matrix is useful to put inward and outward flows into perspective and as a check on the plausibility of assumptions from each side. Although the EC is the fastest growing region for inward investment over this period, its own *outward* investments are still larger than inward flows by a factor of 1.6. European companies as a group invest 50% more abroad than do Japanese companies and more than twice as much as US companies. Europeans become the largest investors in one another's economies, with total inflows twice as large as those coming into the EC from either Japan or the United States. American companies invest about a third of their total outflow in the EC (down from 45% in past decades) and 4% in Japan (roughly the same as in the past).

This scenario is no more than one possible development of FDI flows over the next five years. It is not a prediction. The theory of what motivates such flows does not lend itself to clear or simple statistical prediction and the data are not adequate for complex multi-country models. The quantification is an attempt to impose a consistent framework for inward and outward flows onto a set of assumptions whose plausibility is examined in both historical and cross-country contexts. It tries to use all the data that are available to create a credible picture of what the future may hold.

The result by 1995 is a near doubling of current flows, which themselves have quadrupled since 1983. The greatest activity is in Europe, led by a wave of intra-European mergers, acquisitions and new investments. European companies themselves become the most active international investors. FDI continues to flow into the US but the pace slackens from the 1980s. For the first time Japan is exposed to a rapid growth of inward investment. Flows to – and within – the rest of the world increase, helping to develop Eastern Europe, and strengthening multilateral ties across regions and possibly between north and south. As a force for economic integration and inter-dependence, direct investment gains its place alongside trade.

4

GLOBAL COMPANIES AND TRADE

A basic theme of this paper is that new analytical tools are needed to measure and understand the linkages among advanced economies. The original economic theories of international trade were developed on the assumption of factor immobility; i.e., that land, labour, capital and entrepreneurship stayed within national boundaries while the outputs they combined to produce were traded across borders for mutual gain. In such a world, trade statistics had a well-defined meaning and were a good measure of economic interdependence among countries. But today, trade measures that exclude the role of FOFs in reaching foreign markets are increasingly partial and misleading as indicators of national competitiveness or fundamental trends in the world economy.

The essential idea of comparative advantage and the gains from trade that it makes possible remain valid. Indeed, these gains are reinforced, not dissipated, by foreign direct investment, and many of the FDI policy recommendations in the next chapter are derived from trade policy principles. But comparative advantage is a 'territorial' concept, applicable to regions, countries, hemispheres, etc.; it is not a 'national' concept. The relevant policy concern of national governments is competitiveness. It is a 'national' concept in that it has to do with the ability of national enterprises, including their foreign affiliates, to make their way in global markets with their own products, processes and managerial skills. The changing structure of global industry has created a widening gap between these two concepts. What we need to do is distinguish clearly between comparative advantage on the one hand and industry or national competitiveness on the other. Traditional trade measures (e.g. imports, exports, the balance of payments) focus only on the former. This chapter develops some 'ownership-based' trade measures that shed light on the latter.

The influence of global companies through foreign direct investment could be traced on a whole range of measures: trade flows, interest-profit-dividend (IPD) flows, equity flows to developing countries, domestic currency demand, exchange rate behaviour, capital markets and even labour markets. Much more research on and refinement of the concepts discussed below is needed to formulate such a comprehensive picture. But the basic ideas can be demonstrated by focusing on the largest real economy linkage – namely, trade – and on the key financial linkage – the exchange rate. The availability of data limits the empirical side of this chapter mostly to the United States and Japan.

FDI-related trade

It was shown in Chapter 3 that foreign-owned firms are responsible for a greater share of their host country's exports and imports than of its sales or investment. They are more active as international traders than are their domestic counterparts. Now let's examine this phenomenon from another perspective. How much of a country's recorded trade actually represents purchases/sales by FOFs from/to their home countries? Such 'internal' transactions which arise because of earlier investment flows to establish the FOFs are termed FDI-related trade, defined as cross-border transactions between FOFs and their home countries.*

The concept can easily be understood by considering a two-country world, as shown in Figure 4.1. Both Country 1 and Country 2 contain domestically owned firms, represented by areas A and C, and foreign-owned firms, represented by areas B and D. The firms in B belong to parent firms in C, while firms in A own those in D. We define AB to mean sales by A to B.

FDI-related trade between the two countries of Figure 4.1 can be

---

*FDI-related trade differs from the more common concept of intra-firm trade in that it includes all trade between the FOF and the home country and not just trade between the FOF and the parent firm. Thus the transaction of a French oil company investing in the North Sea and selling its output into the French market would show up as FDI-related trade whether or not the petrol stations in France were owned by that oil company.

Figure 4.1   A two-country world with foreign-owned firms

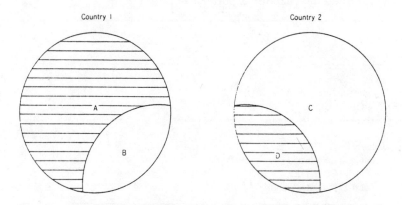

Key: A = Domestically owned firms and consumers in Country 1.
        B = Foreign-owned firms in Country 1.
        C = Domestically owned firms and consumers in Country 2.
        D = Foreign-owned firms in Country 2.

defined in terms of flows between the lettered areas. For Country 1, FDI-related exports are AD and BC. If Country 1 is the US, then AD represents shipments from US firms to US-owned firms abroad, and BC represents sales by FOFs in the US back to their home countries. FDI-related imports include DA, purchases by US companies from US-owned firms abroad, and CB, purchases by FOFs in the US from their home countries.*

The extent to which a country's trade is FDI-related will depend on the size and propensity to trade of its own MNEs abroad and on those it hosts. The US and Japan are quite different in these respects, making their comparison particularly instructive. The US has a larger overseas network of FOFs and, at the same time, smaller export flows relative to GNP than does Japan. The two countries have similar ratios of imports to GNP, but the US is a host to many more FOFs than is Japan.

*In the empirical sections that follow, the data used to estimate FDI-related trade also include transactions that would be labelled BD and DB. This is because the data from the host country on FOFs do not distinguish between foreign- and domestically owned firms in the home country with which its FOFs transact business. While this may introduce some bias into the estimates, both BD and DB are likely to be small, and they are subtracted from each other in the net figures. An example would be a purchase by IBM in Japan from a US-based Hitachi plant.

Table 4.1 FDI-related trade
(% of total merchandise exports or imports)

	US (1986)	Japan (1983)
Exports:		
To affiliates abroad (AD + BD)*	32	38
By FOFs (BC + BD)	23	3
Total FDI-related exports	55	41
Imports:		
From affiliates abroad (DA + DB)*	18	40
To FOFs (CB + DB)	34	17
Total FDI-related imports	52	57

Sources: MITI; US Commerce Department; author's calculations.
*Both BD and DB are likely to be close to zero. To the extent that such trade exists, it will result in double-counting when the two components of FDI-related exports (or imports) are added.

Table 4.1 summarizes the available data on FDI-related trade for the US and Japan. For the US, one-third of its exports go to US-owned firms abroad, while another quarter are by FOFs in the US which are shipping goods back to their home country. In total, 55% of US exports are FDI-related. On the import side, nearly one-fifth of US imports come from US-owned firms abroad and a further one-third are by FOFs in the US receiving goods from their home countries. Japanese-based FOFs export very little but account for 17% of Japan's total imports. Japanese-owned firms abroad are the recipients of 38% of its exports and ship back to Japan 40% of its imports. Thus for both countries, despite their clearly different positions as international investors and as host economies, FDI-related trade already accounts for about half of total trade.

Although it is not possible to find the same figures from published sources for other countries, a partial picture can be obtained by using US data to look at bilateral trade flows. These suggest that FDI-related trade may be an even larger portion of total trade for countries that are smaller than the US and Japan. Table 4.2 shows the percentages of US imports from certain countries and regions that come from US-owned companies in those exporting countries.

Table 4.2 US imports from US-owned firms abroad, 1986
(as a percentage of total US imports from each region)

Canada	43
Japan	9
Europe	11
Australia, New Zealand and South Africa	14
Latin America	19
Other Africa (incl. Middle East)	22
Other Asia and Pacific	12

Source: US Commerce Department.

The extreme case of Canada shows how the operations of an integrated global company can complicate the interpretation of trade figures. The US-Canada Automotive Agreement (since superseded by the US-Canada Free Trade Agreement) allows US car companies to produce on both sides of the border without paying tariffs to either government. This has led US companies to invest and produce in Canada for sales in the US. In 1986 Canada's total exports to the US were valued at $70 billion, of which $30 billion came from US-owned companies in Canada selling back into their home market. At the same time, total US exports to Canada were valued at $57 billion, of which $32 billion represented partially finished goods sent by US companies to their Canadian subsidiaries. Direct investment in this one industry accounted for half of total trade between the two countries. The long-term impact on trade of the US-Canada Free Trade Agreement could be much larger than has been projected if it provokes many US and Canadian companies to follow the example of automobiles.

In most other regions or countries, exports by US-owned companies back to the US are a smaller share of total US imports than in Canada. However, for some developing countries the share is even higher. To cite two extreme examples, in 1982, 47% of US imports from Singapore and 52% from Malaysia were from US affiliates in those countries, producing mostly electronic equipment. Taiwan's five leading electronics exporters are US-owned firms. A recently published study from Australia showed that five of that country's ten largest exporters were Japanese-owned firms, and only nine of the top 20 exporters were Australian-owned companies (*Australian Business*, 1989). The large flows of Japanese FDI into the Asian

75

NIEs and ASEAN over the last five years are likely to result in a major increase in FDI-related exports from those countries over the next decade. Thus FDI-related trade is even more dominant in some developing countries than it is in the US and Japan.

Local sales and purchases by FOFs

We have seen above that much of the cross-border flow of goods and services that are recorded as trade between countries actually represents 'internal' transactions between FOFs and their country of ownership. Now we look at the other side of this coin. From the point of view of the firm, how important are the local sales of its FOFs abroad, compared with exports, as a way to reach foreign consumers? And how significant are the local purchases of those firms in their host economies, compared with imports, as a way of sourcing foreign inputs and factors of production?

For Country 1 in Figure 4.1, local sales of FOFs are represented by BA and local purchases by AB. These transactions do not show up at all in traditional trade measures because no cross-border flow of goods or money takes place. From the viewpoint of the firm, however, a local sale (BA) by a subsidiary abroad is as much a 'foreign sale' as is an export (CA). Similarly, a local purchase by that subsidiary (AB) is as much a 'foreign purchase' as is an import (AC).

How large are the local sales and purchases of FOFs relative to trade flows? For the largest host country, the United States, the total sales of FOFs located there were 150% of total US imports in 1985. A more detailed breakdown shows that, for 11 of the 12 largest OECD countries, the local sales of their firms in the US were larger than US imports from that country. In Germany local sales by FOFs were 139% of total German imports. Even for Japan, the country with the lowest penetration of FOFs, their local sales are 42% of the country's imports. In other words, nearly 30% of the 'foreign purchases' (i.e., including both imports and purchases from FOFs in Japan) made by Japanese consumers are from the few FOFs operating in Japan.

More detailed information on the export side is available from US statistics (see Table 4.3). Since the US is the largest and most established international investor, the local sales of its MNEs overseas are likely to be larger, relative to its exports, than is the case for most other countries. Nonetheless, it is striking that for nearly all

Table 4.3 Local sales by US-owned companies in each country compared with US exports to that country, 1986

	Ratio of local sales to US exports
Total	1.15
Canada	1.99
Japan	1.11
Mexico	0.51
UK	6.76
Germany	4.97
Netherlands	1.75
France	4.91
Australia	3.68
Taiwan	0.26
Italy	4.85
Brazil	5.10
Singapore	0.48
Venezuela	0.80
Hong Kong	1.04

Note: Countries listed in order of absolute size of US exports to the country.

of its major trading partners, local sales by US firms abroad are larger than US exports to the country.

Unfortunately, the same kinds of figures are not available for the local purchases of FOFs. However, it is possible to construct an estimate of their magnitude from the information on FOFs shown in Table 3.2. In the US, FOFs account for 10% of gross sales and 34% of US imports. Total US imports are 12% of its GNP. If the ratio of gross sales to value added (which is how GNP is measured) is the same for foreign-owned and domestic firms in the US, then FOFs will also account for 10% of GNP. The imports of FOFs then will equal 4% of GNP (0.12 x 0.34). This implies a 'local content' of 60% in their production $[1-(0.04/0.10)]$.* Meanwhile, similar calculations show that the 'local content' for domestic firms in the US would be 91%.

*The meaning of local content in this section is not the same as its meaning in EC anti-dumping actions. Here it includes everything not imported; ie, the firm's labour, electricity and other non-material local costs, as well as locally procured materials and profits.

For Japan, imports represent 10% of GNP, while FOFs account for 17% of total imports and only slightly more than 1% of gross sales. This implies the same 'local content' for domestic firms as in the US – 91% – but less than 5% 'local content' for FOFs in Japan. This very low figure looks suspect. No direct confirmation is possible because the Japanese government does not collect such information from FOFs operating there. For lack of a better estimate, the 5% figure is used in the calculations in the next section, but it may be too low and, in any case, it is likely to increase as inward investment in Japan accelerates.

An alternative measure of 'trade'
We are now ready to construct an alternative measure of the economic linkages between countries. This measure should include both ways of reaching foreign markets – through exports/imports and through the local sales/purchases of FOFs. However, it must not double-count the FDI-related trade which could show up as both. For example, if Honda US imports automobile engines from Japan, installs them in its US-assembled cars and then sells the cars locally, the engines could be double-counted since they are included both in Japan's exports to the US and in the local sales of Japanese-owned firms in the US.

The organizing principle is to convert traditional import and export figures into measures of 'foreign purchases' and 'foreign sales' which assign transactions according to nationality of ownership rather than residency. The intent is to create a measure that reflects the fact that a firm can choose to supply a foreign market either by exporting to it or by investing in it and selling locally. Such ownership-based measures should be insensitive to shifts in foreign strategy by individual firms.

The basic procedure is to subtract FDI-related trade from the traditional trade measures (to avoid double-counting) and to add the local sales/purchases of FOFs. This is most easily explained by referring back to Figure 4.1 and the terminology introduced above. The exports of Country 1 on the traditional residence basis (X_{1R}) can be written as:

$$X_{1R} = (AC + AD) + (BC + BD).$$

Country 1's exports on an ownership basis (X_{1O}) would include all foreign sales by A and D, thus:

Figure 4.2   Summary matrix of residence- and ownership-based trade measures

From	To			
	A	B	C	D
A	—	O	R, O	R
B	O	—	R	R, O
C	R, O	R	—	O
D	R	R, O	O	—

$$X_{IO} = (AC + AB) + (DC + DB).$$

Imports (M) are defined in a symmetric way:

$$M_{IR} = (CA + DA) + (CB + DB) \text{ and}$$
$$M_{IO} = (CA + BA) + (CD + BD).$$

The relationship between residence-based measures and ownership-based measures is summarized in Figure 4.2. A cell with 'R' indicates that transactions between the coordinates of that cell are included in the residence-based measure; 'R,O' signifies inclusion in both measures and 'O' in the ownership-based measure.

In two of the cells, BD and DB, the transaction is included in both residence- and ownership-based trade measures, but in one case the sale is considered an export, while in the other it is an import. This is the most counterintuitive element of the ownership-based measures; i.e., when a good crossing the border into a country is considered an 'export' of that country. What is important on an ownership basis is the change of country of ultimate ownership of the good, not its change of location. Although these two cells highlight the difference in the two measures more starkly than the others, in practice both BD and DB are probably insignificant, as mentioned above.

We can now use the concepts discussed above to transform the traditional residence-based trade measures into ownership-based ones. Rather than using the terms exports and imports, it is perhaps better to think of these as foreign sales and foreign purchases where the difference between the two trade measures hinges on the definition of foreign. For residence-based measures, foreign means across the border, regardless of ownership. For ownership-based measures, foreign refers to the dominant ownership of the firm making the sale. This concept is not always unambiguous with truly global companies whose 'home' market may account for a small percentage of total sales or profits. This and other limitations of the ownership-based measures are discussed in the next section.

The ownership-based measure of foreign sales for Country 1 (X_{1O}) can be expressed in terms of its residence-based measure (X_{1R}) as follows:

$$X_{1O} = X_{1R} - (AD + BC) + (AB + DC) - (BD - DB)$$

The first set of parentheses is the FDI-related trade included in X_{1R}. The second set includes the local sales by Country 1's firms and workers to FOFs in Country 1 (AB) and the local sales of its own firms in their host economies (DC). The final set of parentheses represents transactions between FOFs abroad and those in their home countries, which is assumed to be zero both for imports and for exports. Data on it are not available, but this assumption is unlikely to introduce a significant or systematic distortion to the estimates developed below. Ownership-based foreign purchases (M_{1O}) can be expressed in terms of their residence-based counterpart (M_{1R}) in a similar way:

$$M_{1O} = M_{1R} - (DA + CB) + (BA + CD) - (DB - BD).$$

Table 4.4 shows the estimates of ownership-based trade measures for the US and Japan in terms of these components. For the United States, foreign sales (X_O) are more than five times as large as exports (X_R), while foreign purchases (M_O) are almost three times as large as imports (M_R). Thus the ownership-based measures show a much greater degree of integration of the US economy with the rest of the world than do traditional trade measures. For Japan, foreign sales are 1.7 times exports and foreign purchases are 1.7 times imports. Despite its large trade presence, the smaller degree of integration of the Japanese economy, relative to the US, comes through in its ownership-based measures. Foreign sales represented 27% of US gross national product in 1986, compared with 21% for Japan in

Table 4.4 Ownership-based trade measures for the US and Japan (US $ bn)

	US (1986)	Japan (1983)
Foreign sales		
Exports (X_R)	224.0	145.7
less: FDI-related exports		
to FOFs abroad (AD)	71.7	55.4
by local FOFs (BC)	51.5	4.4
plus: Local sales		
to local FOFs (AB)*	267.0	2.9
by FOFs abroad (DC)	777.0	150.0
Total foreign sales (X_o)	1,144.8	238.8
Foreign purchases		
Imports (M_R)	368.4	114.1
less: FDI-related imports		
by FOFs abroad (DA)	66.3	45.6
to local FOFs (CB)	125.2	19.4
plus: local purchases		
from local FOFs (BA)	445.0	58.0
by FOFs abroad (CD)	446.2	90.0
Total foreign purchases (M_o)	1,088.1	197.1
Net foreign sales ($X_o - M_o$)	+56.7	+41.7
Net exports ($X_R - M_R$)	-144.4	+31.6

*Estimated from the local content figures discussed in the text: 5% for FOFs in Japan, 60% for FOFs in the US, and 60% for both US and Japanese firms in all other markets.

1983. In the same years, US exports were 5.3% of GNP while Japanese exports were 12% of its GNP.

The ownership-based figures also provide a broader measure of the international competitiveness of US and Japanese companies whose presence in global markets comes both through FDI and through trade. While the figures themselves are too imprecise to warrant detailed comparison, it is striking that the 1986 US trade balance is transformed from a deficit of $144 billion on a residence basis (net exports) to a surplus of $57 billion on an ownership basis (net foreign sales). Japan's 1983 trade surplus widens slightly on an ownership basis, from net exports of $32 billion to net foreign sales of $42 billion.*

Because of the broader coverage of the ownership-based figures, they should show more stability over time. The major effort that Japanese companies are making to shift production overseas – both for the home market and for export markets – was discussed in Chapter 2. Such a shift would be accommodated in the ownership-based measures, while it could cause the residence-based measures to lurch dramatically despite there being no fundamental change in the competitiveness of Japanese companies. Indeed, there have already been complaints that the success of Japanese efforts to reduce their trade surplus by increasing imports of manufactures has largely come about through imports from Japanese-owned companies in other East Asian countries. The problem with this argument is not that it is untrue, but that it assumes that changes in the trade balance still reflect fundamental shifts in competitiveness.

Once the key factors of production are mobile, and the optimal management area for many industries is multinational, then it is inevitable that the measures of competitiveness must change. As the industrial structure of advanced economies has changed from agriculture to manufacturing to services, what is most important to competitive success is no longer a country's land and mineral endowment or even, in many cases, its labour costs. Rather it is a whole range of non-geographical factors: access to technology, flexible management techniques, marketing strategy, closeness to consumers, speed of response to changes in the market-place, etc. All of these are firm-specific, not territorially based. None of them can be built overnight, in the way that capital can now be raised or unskilled labour hired. Industrial organization theory tells us that multinationals develop because of the presence of a firm-specific asset. This asset – perhaps in-house technology or a style of management – is often intangible and non-tradable. It is in the nature of a public good in that once it is created it can be used for low or zero marginal cost by other parts of the firm. Yet the services of the asset – the licensing of technology or the reputation behind a

---

*On a global basis, foreign sales must equal foreign purchases. Thus some countries would find their ownership balance to be in deficit while the trade balance is in surplus. Although no figures are available, it is likely that Germany would show a much smaller surplus on an ownership basis than on a residence basis, because it is an important host economy to FOFs while having a relatively low stock of overseas direct investments.

company name – cannot be traded well at arm's length. Under such imperfectly competitive conditions, multinational firms develop to exploit the assets that the market cannot otherwise tap. Dunning calls such intangible assets ownership advantages (1977), while other researchers have other names for them or other ways of describing them (Batra and Ramachandran, 1980; Deardorff, 1985; Helpman, 1984, 1985; Markusen, 1984).*

The advanced economies have now reached a point where these two sets of theory – trade and the industrial organization of MNEs – must be brought together through the development of new analytical tools. Changes in consumer demand and industrial structure mean that more and more of a country's consumption and production is dependent on intangible assets, be it technology or consumer services. These can best be developed and sold to other countries' consumers by MNEs with a foreign presence through direct investment. It follows that statistical concepts which are based on territorial definitions cannot provide the comprehensive indicators of underlying competitive trends that analysts and policy-makers need.

Limitations of the analysis

The case for new analytical tools is clear. The ownership-based trade measures developed in this chapter are an initial effort in that direction. Their purpose is to demonstrate the size of the gap between traditional measures and ones which try to capture economic interdependence more comprehensively. They are limited by data on the activities of MNEs for countries other than the US and Japan. However, there are also conceptual problems that must be addressed.

First, if ownership is to be the basic criterion for sorting transactions into their foreign and domestic components, then we need a definition of ownership that corresponds to where the firm's profit-maximizing decisions are being taken – i.e., to where control is being exercised. This has two dimensions: nationality of ownership and style of management. On the ownership question, the nationality of a global company could mean: (i) the country where it is legally established; (ii) the country where its headquarters is located; (iii) the dominant nationality of its shareholders; (iv) the dominant nationality of its board of directors; (v) the dominant nationality of its

*For a review of this work, see Thomsen (1990).

workforce; or even (vi) the dominant market into which it sells or from which it earns the bulk of its profits. An Anglo-Saxon economist would choose (iii) as the best criterion. A German or Japanese economist – and most politicians – would prefer (v). A lawyer might plump for (i) or (ii). A management consultant would like (vi). And the board of directors of the company itself would claim that its goal is to be truly multinational – or, as the Japanese now call it, globally localized – and that the attempt to pin a country label on it is a complete misrepresentation.

This brings us to the question of management style. In some global companies – Shell is one – decentralization of decision-making is so ingrained that even wholly owned subsidiaries are very much their own master in their own environment. By contrast, Exxon is tightly managed from the centre and resources are actively traded off across country divisions. Such differences in company philosophy may affect how the host country benefits from FDI in terms of its stability and spin-offs for the local economy. Clearly it also has an influence on control – on where the profit-maximizing decisions are taken.

The nationality issue is a complex one and it is becoming more so with the surge in FDI in this decade. Company accounts attest to this without necessarily providing enlightenment on the central question. What is meant by a Bahamas-registered company 'repatriating' its profits? Should one assume ultimate US ownership? What would be the appropriate designation of United Airlines if it came to be 29% owned by British Airways, 30% of whose shareholders were US residents? Should company nationality be defined by an arithmetic calculation or does it have a more fundamental meaning?

As with most social science questions, the right definition is the one that fits the problem being addressed. The main concern of this study is to understand how the recent wave of foreign direct investment affects the linkages among economies. Since those linkages weave through trade measures but also act directly through transactions that are not counted as trade, we require a different approach to data collection based on different definitional categories. However, as long as the limited aims of this exercise are understood, we do not need to delve into the philosophical issues of company nationality that would have to be faced if it were suggested that governments enact policies that differentiated between 'national' and 'foreign' firms. In fact, Chapter 5 explicitly counsels *against* such policies, although on more fundamental grounds than problems of definition.

For the purpose of this study, the advice of the Anglo-Saxon economist is taken: company ownership is determined by the dominant nationality of its shareholders. In practice, this will nearly always coincide with criterion (iv), the dominant nationality of its board of directors – which is often easier to establish. The board-room remains a bastion yet to be stormed by 'foreigners', long after companies have gone for multiple listings on foreign stock exchanges, for worldwide sourcing and distribution, for the presentation of company accounts in ECU or SDRs, and for international recruitment programmes for executives. And, in any fundamental sense, only people have nationalities.

A definition based on shareholder nationality is consistent with the interpretation of takeover actions and with the legal obligations of the company directors to act in the interests of the shareholders. Unfortunately this new definition does not correspond with the data as they are now collected. The recommended practice is to count the purchase of a 10% stake as foreign direct investment and to consider the company which receives the investment as having 'foreign ownership' even if 90% of its shares remain in domestic hands.

For balance-of-payments purposes, the IMF/OECD cut-off of 10% ownership is a sensible threshold to divide direct investment from portfolio investment. The idea behind this division is that direct investment is an autonomous flow reflecting long-term commercial considerations while portfolio investment is a short-term balancing item that responds to financial market variables such as interest rates and exchange rate expectations.

With integrated capital markets and floating exchange rates, however, the balance of payments has lost its former role as the authoritative summary of a country's external position. It is merely one way of sorting economic transactions into categories that present a balance sheet of residence-based, currency-specific trade and capital flows. It is no longer a very meaningful way of analysing international economic linkages or fundamental questions about the wealth of nations.

At the national level, we need to reorganize – or, in many countries, initiate – data collection on the sales and purchases of multinational companies. For this information, the reporting threshold should be raised from 10% to 50% foreign ownership. No

distinction would be made between greenfield and takeover investment, nor between that locally financed and that which involved
FDI. For those countries which already collect information on
FOFs, raising the threshold would reduce the coverage of existing
surveys and remove a reporting burden from predominantly
domestic firms. At the same time, however, the industry coverage
needs to be expanded in many cases. In many of the European
countries it is still limited to the manufacturing sector, when over
half of FDI is in services. In the US foreign investment in the
financial sector is treated differently from that elsewhere. A comprehensive and consistent approach across sectors, but limited to firms
with 50% or greater foreign ownership, would be a major improvement on current practice and would bring cost savings, in many
cases, to governments and companies.

In addition to new reporting requirements for FOFs at home, the
governments of the main outward-investing countries should coordinate their data collection on the international activities of their
own MNEs. Again the aim should be to reduce to a minimum
reporting requirements or survey length, while increasing the cross-
sectoral coverage of the data. The biggest outward investor, the
United States, has a fairly good system in place to provide it with
data on the foreign sales of American companies in their host
markets. Japan has recently begun collecting such information from
its companies, although its coverage and definitions are not identical
with those used by the US. Other large international investors –
notably Britain – do not collect such data.

Given the size and recent growth of overseas investment by British
companies, information on their sales and purchase activities
abroad would clearly be of great interest. An analysis carried out by
a London brokerage house on those companies listed on the Stock
Exchange showed that the average proportion of their profits earned
through exports had fallen from 16% in 1978 to 5% in 1987. Over
the same period the proportion of profits coming from overseas sales
by their subsidiaries rose to reach 39% – nearly eight times exports –
by 1987 (Phillips and Drew, 1988). Under these conditions, to focus
on the current account when trying to assess the strength of the
British economy is clearly misleading (Julius, 1987). But the government – and the markets – lack the data to support a broader look.

Finally, it is important to be clear about what ownership-based
trade measures do *not* mean. They are an alternative to – rather than

a replacement for – the traditional residence-based balance-of-payments measures. Because they do not measure cross-border economic flows *per se*, they would be of little use in monitoring or interpreting the external situation of a developing country – or an East European country – with a foreign exchange constraint. Where a country's currency is not freely convertible or where there are foreign exchange controls, then a residence-based, currency-specific set of measures is a better guide to the need for policy action to support the exchange rate or to reschedule debt. The problem arises when such traditional measures are given undue attention in economies which are fully integrated into global capital markets and for which foreign exchange is not a binding constraint but has a price like all others.

Implications for exchange rates
The system of fixed exchange rates set up after World War II at Bretton Woods collapsed more than 15 years ago. Yet the mentality behind it survives, not least in the way we structure economic accounts. The figures which those accounts provide, month after month, guide the behaviour of governments and financial market participants in ways that sometimes diverge substantially from the economic fundamentals, as perceived by actors in the real economy where goods and services are produced, traded and consumed.

Those actors have diversified their operations across markets, achieving a closer match between costs and revenues in major currency areas. They have grown more resistant to exchange rate swings and more flexible in avoiding their adverse effects. Widespread international operations with high local content provide shelter in foreign markets which simple export operations lack.

This has macroeconomic repercussions. The current account balance is no longer the tail that wags the dog for a big, integrated economy whose firms are selling much more abroad through their subsidiaries than they are routeing through the export column of their country's balance of payments. The United States is a case in point. A widespread and enduring consensus developed among economists and policy-makers in the US, Europe and Japan that the twin deficits of the US budget and current account constituted the biggest single threat to continued world economic growth (IIE, 1987). Yet recent experience suggests that a large and continuing

87

external deficit, under a system of floating exchange rates, can be quite sustainable. The external debt of the US is growing more slowly than its economy, the budget deficit is shrinking as a proportion of GNP and the buoyancy of corporate profits during the mid-1980s (when deficits were largest) suggests that, at the microeconomic level, the rate of return on investment was considerably higher than the interest rates which were necessary to attract the foreign capital that financed the current account deficit. Seen from this perspective, it makes little sense to claim that a fall in the dollar is the inevitable consequence of – and the necessary condition to correct – the continuing external deficit.

But even if the deficit can be sustained on a flow basis, isn't the growing stock of foreign debt that it implies a major worry? Recent research at the US Federal Reserve Board examined the future servicing burden created by the accumulating US indebtedness to foreigners (Stekler and Helkie, 1989). The researchers began with the paradox that although the US became a net debtor sometime in 1985, its net investment income (i.e., the interest and dividends it receives from abroad less those it pays to foreigners) has remained positive. Owing to various anomalies in the way that US external assets are measured – including the undervaluation of US direct investment which is held at its book value and the omission of most US deposits in foreign banks – and the empirical fact that US residents have long earned a higher rate of return on their assets abroad than foreigners earn on their assets in the United States, the authors refute the remaining concern of the doomsayers that the growing US debt is a gathering storm-cloud on the horizon:

> Our simulations of future US net investment income payments indicate that the servicing burden imposed by continued and growing US indebtedness to foreigners over the next decade is likely to be surprisingly small and slow-growing relative to the size of the US economy. If not for growing US international indebtedness, the United States would tend to show a growing surplus on net investment income. Investors' willingness to continue to lend to the United States at current interest and exchange rates is likely to be influenced by many factors in addition to their assessments of the ability of the United States to service its growing debt. However, based only on the narrow assessment of the likely small size of the future servicing

burden, there would appear to be little reason for investors to be overly concerned. (Stekler and Helkie, 1989)

The US is not the only country for which the current account position is a misleading indicator of economic health and the sustainability of present policies and exchange rates. The situation in the UK is, in some respects, even more striking. As a *Financial Times* leader put it in August 1989 just after the publication of the second largest monthly trade deficit in Britain's history, 'The more the UK borrows, the richer it gets.' Although the UK ran a current account deficit of nearly £15 billion in 1988, its net external asset position *increased* from £90 billion to £94 billion over the course of the year. This feat was possible essentially because, first, the UK's external asset base is very large, relative even to the big annual deficit it ran; and, second, the market value of UK assets abroad rose faster than that of foreign assets in the UK. For the UK, 'to be a net borrower of financial assets and a net investor in a diversified portfolio of real assets has once more proved profitable' (*FT*, 24.8.89). The analogy with a corporate balance sheet is clear: as long as rates of return on overseas direct investments are higher at the margin than they are at home, it would be folly indeed for Britain Ltd to repatriate its foreign profits (and further overheat the domestic economy) simply for the sake of balancing its current account.

The examples of the US and the UK are extreme ones in that they are the world's largest foreign direct investors. However, as shown in Chapter 2, a plausible scenario can be developed which by 1995 brings Japan's ratio of outward FDI stock to GNP up to the level reached by the US in 1980. Germany and France would exceed the UK's 1980 level by 1995. We are rapidly reaching the point where balance of payments compilations have lost most of their meaning for a large number of advanced economies.

This has two important implications for exchange rates. First, they are a less powerful influence on the real economy than they once were. More than half of trade is FDI-related and thus, as illustrated below, is more resistant to exchange rate movements than are exports. Direct investment has created new avenues into foreign markets which provide a natural hedge against exchange rate losses by a closer matching of revenues and costs in the same currency. Thus when that currency goes down (or up) against the company's base currency, some of the revenue losses (or gains) are automatically offset by savings (or increases) in expenditures. This added immunity to exchange rate risk is one reason that companies give for preferring a diversified base of operations. Although it has probably not been a major factor behind the FDI surge of the 1980s, the unintended effect is a more stable world economy, one which is more resistant to swings in financial markets. This added stability and resistance provided by the FDI linkage has been an important explanation of the long-running economic expansion of the 1980s.

To see how serving a foreign market through FDI rather than through exports makes a company more resistant to adverse movements in exchange rates, consider the following example. Suppose British Bicycles Ltd can produce a bicycle for £100 which it can export to France and sell for 1100 francs. At an exchange rate of £1 = ff10, this yields a unit profit for British Bicycles of £10 (ff1100 = £110; £110 − £100 = £10). Now suppose the franc depreciates by 10% against the pound so that the exchange rate is £1 = ff11. The bicycle market in France is a competitive one with several domestic manufacturers, so British Bicycles Ltd cannot raise the price of its bicycles in France without losing market share. If it continues to sell them for ff1100, its unit profit will be reduced to zero (ff1100 = £100; £100 − £100 = 0). A 10% shift in exchange rates has wiped out its profit on overseas sales via export. Under these circumstances it might decide to stop serving the French market.

Now suppose that instead of exporting its bicycles, British Bicycles Ltd sets up a French subsidiary to assemble its bicycles for the French market in France. It exports bicycle parts to its subsidiary worth £40 and the subsidiary incurs the rest of the costs (£60) locally. (To keep things simple, there is assumed to be no difference in labour or other production costs between the two countries.) In the initial period when the exchange rate is £1 = ff10, these local costs are thus ff600. When the bicycle is sold for ff1100, the profits of the French subsidiary (ff1100 − ff600 = ff500) are remitted to its British parent. This produces the same £10 profit as in the export case (ff500 = £50; £50 − £40 = £10). Now the French franc depreciates to £1 = ff11. The local costs of the French subsidiary do not change, so ff500 is still remitted to the UK. At the new exchange rate this is worth only £45.45, leaving a unit profit of £5.45 (£45.45 − £40 = £5.45). Through its strategy of FDI, British Bicycles Ltd has retained over half of its profit in the face of an adverse shift in exchange rates, compared with the export case where the profits were wiped out. It is likely to continue serving the French market.

This example illustrates how market integration through FDI rather than through trade softens the influence – decreases the power – of exchange rates on the real-economy variables that matter, such as production, investment and employment. Firms serving foreign markets through local subsidiaries can withstand large swings in exchange rates more easily and are more resistant to persistent over- or under-valuations of the major trading currencies. Thus market integration through FDI acts to de-link the real economy from movements in financial markets. The second implication for exchange rates is that, left to their own devices, they will become more volatile. This follows partly from the first implication. Because their interaction with the real economy has weakened, exchange rates have lost much of the 'grounding' they once had as prices which equilibrated real flows of goods across borders. Without this grounding, and with the greatly increased volume of foreign exchange trading under the post-Bretton Woods floating rate regime, exchange rates are buffeted by the financial markets in the same way as are share prices or commodity futures.

Economists sometimes refer to a country's fundamental equilibrium exchange rate (FEER), which is the unique value of the currency, on a trade weighted basis, that causes the current account and long-term capital flows to balance over time. If it now turns out that there is a range – say, plus or minus 40% – around the FEER that can yield a sustainable balance-of-payments position, then the suggestion that countries return to a system of fixed-but-adjustable exchange rates maintained by central bank intervention in order to be equal to their respective FEERs would be like binding a healthy athlete with a paper strait-jacket: both ineffective and unnecessary.

Yet even under a floating exchange rate regime, it may well be in the interests of a particular country – especially a relatively small, open one – to aim for greater exchange rate stability by tying itself to a larger buoy. After all, a corollary of the first implication, the weakened influence of the exchange rate on the real economy, is that it will become less useful to governments as a tool to stimulate growth or reduce unemployment. Exchange rate changes by them-selves have less impact on external imbalances than they used to have. A depreciation of the currency to improve competitiveness is less likely to work, and may even be counterproductive by inducing inflation. And if exchange rates become both less important and more volatile, then an arrangement like the European Monetary System provides a sheltered haven with few costs, even if one joins at a rate which in retrospect turns out to have been a few pence off the FEER.

5

IMPLICATIONS FOR PUBLIC POLICY

The preceding chapters have documented the multiplying and deepening linkages among national markets created by direct investment and the growth of foreign sales and purchases that it brings. This process of FDI-led market integration is analogous to the financial integration that took place from the mid-1970s to the mid-1980s. It too had a variety of causes: the breakdown of Bretton Woods, the oil-induced shock of high inflation, the liberalization of domestic financial markets and the information technology revolution, to name a few. It resulted in a global financial market, transmitting shocks across borders instantaneously, 24 hours a day, and in the effective disappearance of national financial boundaries. Will FDI-led integration of real markets result in a global economy and the demise of national economic borders? And what sorts of policy choices will governments make along the way?

The experience of financial market integration provides several useful lessons. The first is that as markets integrate across borders, the ability of national policies to influence the structure of the market or the behaviour of market participants is greatly reduced. Side-channels multiply, and slippages and lags are created between a policy change and the market response. Sometimes the new side-channels permit adverse impacts. For example, to curtail its inflation a country may tighten its monetary policy by raising domestic interest rates. If its financial markets are insulated from the rest of the world, this will have the desired effect by restraining the growth of the money supply and depressing investment. However, if its financial markets are open, the higher interest rates may simply attract capital from abroad thereby expanding the domestic money supply and stimulating investment. Indeed, much of the disillusion felt by economists who embraced monetarism in the 1970s can be traced to the fact that national money demand functions have lost their empirical stability in the 1980s with the integration of capital markets and the proliferation of near-money instruments (Frowen, 1990).

Chapter 4 showed how a similar erosion is taking place in the power of the exchange rate as a national policy tool. This is partly because of the side-channel into foreign markets created by FDI that bypasses the export route, converting neither costs nor profits into the home currency. But the loss of national policy autonomy extends beyond financial and currency markets. Global companies have at least a limited ability to shift their internal pricing systems and, over the long run, even their operations to avoid high-tax environments or onerous government reporting requirements.

This leads to the second lesson from financial market integration: a powerful internal dynamic is created for policy convergence across countries. At the microeconomic level, market integration means that firms which used to compete with other national firms under their common national rules now find themselves with foreign competitors who operate at home under different rules. Some of the regulatory differences will benefit the home firm; some will penalize it. As global competition intensifies, firms are bound to put pressure on their governments to remove or amend the latter type of regulation. Meanwhile their competitors will urge their own governments to adopt the former type of policies. Such pressures have already led to some convergence of corporate tax rates across the OECD countries. While market-led policy convergence is generally beneficial from a global standpoint, it is an added constraint on national policy-makers.

The third issue that arises for integrated markets is the question of systemic stability. There is a theoretical possibility that pressures in favour of policy convergence will drive the level of regulation so low that the foundations of the market itself are undermined. In banking, for example, this could happen if new banks were allowed to take deposits and make loans without any licensing authority to ensure an adequate capital base and proper protection for consumer deposits. If a few unscrupulous banks were set up and failed, public confidence in the whole banking system could be undermined.

Outside the financial markets, systemic problems could arise where issues of public safety or the environment are involved (an example being chemical additives in foods) or where the market itself may be subject to monopolistic domination and anti-competitive practices. International policy coordination will be required to deal with such systemic problems if they arise. But this is more of a platitude than a panacea. In banking, after 12 years of negotiations through the Bank for International Settlements, the Cooke Committee achieved agreement on a common set of capital adequacy ratios to be applied by bank regulators in the major OECD countries. That such a large effort was required over such a relatively small issue demonstrates the difficulty of the process.

If policy coordination is to succeed, its use must be limited and its aims well focused. It should be attempted only where the problem to be addressed is clearly a systemic one. This creates the incentive for countries to participate since they know they cannot solve the problem alone. Focusing the coordination onto tightly defined areas of policy permits negotiations to be carried out by technical specialists, under the guidance of their political masters but outside the glare of publicity. However, as discussed below, it is not yet clear that FDI-led market integration entails systemic threats. The analogy to a collapse of the financial system would be monopolistic threats to the competitive market system. This is a theoretical possibility under certain types of industrial structure. However, the evidence so far suggests that opening markets to foreign investment stimulates, rather than stifles, competition in the host country.

In sum, the policy pressures of FDI-led market integration are likely to push policy-makers further along the path with which they have grown familiar through financial market integration: spreading liberalization and deregulation of domestic markets and reduced scope for national policy autonomy. This makes it necessary to consider national policies towards inward investment from an international perspective.

Inward investment policy
The scenario developed in Chapters 2 and 3 shows that the stock of

global FDI in 1995 could well be more than double in real terms what it is today. Already inward investment is politically contentious, even in the US and the UK where the official attitude has been welcoming and where domestic firms' holdings of foreign assets are very large. If the healthy development of FDI is to continue, the political debate about it must be better informed. Host-country policies towards inward investment must proceed from clear general principles that are understood and shared across countries.

As background for those principles, it is useful to summarize the conclusions drawn in Chapter 3 about the costs and benefits of inward investment.

(1) There are direct economic benefits from integration through FDI which work through the same channels as gains from trade; i.e., comparative advantage through cross-country specialization, economies of scale, and greater competition. These will be particularly large in the service sectors where integration through trade has been limited both by the nature of the business and by government regulation.

(2) There may be indirect (external) benefits and costs associated with FDI but these are generally impossible to quantify. Thus the balance of benefits over costs or vice versa cannot be assumed *a priori*. If policies could be designed to encourage the indirect benefits and/or minimize the indirect costs, without jeopardizing the overall size of FDI flows and thus their direct benefits, this might be worth doing. However, in advanced economies with many avenues for technology transfer and well-functioning capital markets, these indirect effects of FDI are likely to be much smaller than the direct effects. Policies which distort FDI flows in order to increase indirect net benefits will prove counterproductive if the distortion reduces direct benefits even by a small percentage.

(3) Foreign-owned firms do not behave in a systematically different way from domestic firms. The diversity of management practice and company organization *within* groups of both FOFs and domestic firms is much greater than differences *between* the means of the two groups.

(4) Most advanced countries are big investors in other countries as well as being themselves recipients of FDI. This implies, first, that the scope for retaliation against restrictive policies

towards FOFs cannot be ignored. Second, global companies of whatever origin have many choices on where to expand operations and how inputs and outputs should be moved among plants in different countries. This private sector flexibility acts as a countervailing force to government authority. It makes national policies less effective and increases the chances of perverse results. However, Japan is an important exception to this conclusion: it is host to very little inward investment, and its situation deserves examination as a special case.

General principles

From these four conclusions, two general principles can be derived to provide the basis for evaluating policies towards inward investment. The similarities of these principles to those governing trade policy should not be surprising, given the trade-like nature of FDI both in its motivation and in its multilateral, labyrinthine structure. As with trade, increased international flows of FDI should be encouraged because they bring both global and national benefits. They stimulate growth through more efficient production and they lower prices through greater competition.

These benefits can best be achieved in a policy environment of neutrality, or non-discrimination. In the case of FDI, policy neutrality has two dimensions. The first is identical to that for non-discriminatory trade policy: equal treatment of foreign and domestic firms in the home market. This central principle of 'national treatment' is a simple but deceptively powerful one. It would prohibit, for example, special reporting requirements for foreign-owned firms. It would also prohibit local content requirements, since domestic firms face no such restraints on their choice of inputs.

The second neutrality condition for FDI is that policy should be neutral between trade and investment as alternative vehicles for reaching the target market. This trade/investment neutrality is needed to reap the full efficiency gains of FDI and it has specific implications for market access, as discussed below.

Against the backdrop of these two general principles, one must examine the exceptional cases of FDI that may subvert market processes or threaten other policy objectives. Consider, in turn, the four types of problems that may be associated with FDI, as discussed in Chapter 3: non-economic concerns such as national security; 'strategic' or monopolistic behaviour by FOFs; maximizing the indirect benefits of FDI such as employment creation or technology transfer; and issues of reciprocal market access or a 'level playing field' for takeovers.

Non-economic concerns

First, there are the non-economic concerns over threats to national security or culture posed by foreign takeovers of defence-related industries or parts of the media. What is needed here is an explicit but bounded recognition of these exceptions as legitimate concerns of any government, along with a transparent procedure to vet and either veto or approve FDI on those grounds. The Exon-Floria procedure in the United States comes close to this. By contrast, the authority of the UK's Department of Trade and Industry to block a takeover on 'national interest' grounds is neither bounded nor transparent.

In any case, the national security argument is becoming increasingly outdated for European countries. Economies of scale, driven partly by the high costs of research and development in the defence industries, are pushing them into cross-national mergers and alliances. This makes 'national security' in the old procurement sense a European, rather than a national, issue.

In theory, national – or EC – mechanisms should be augmented by an international court or dispute-settlement procedure to allow one country to challenge the findings of another on grounds of national security or culture. But that route is a long way off and may be rendered unnecessary – by technological developments, the spread of global industries to other sectors and greater cultural exchange – by the time it could be negotiated. The greatest pay-off would be from a reform of the national policies of the major investing countries along the lines proposed.

Strategic behaviour and the use of competition policy

The second, and more difficult, exception to the general principles for open FDI policies concerns the possibility of 'strategic' behaviour by foreign companies or their governments. This is analogous to trade policy concerns over dumping to take advantage of economies of scale or over government subsidies and other forms of 'unfair' industrial policy. The practical and political difficulties of dealing with such fears, even if they are justified, are enormous. In this case, to pattern FDI policy on trade policy techniques would compound a felony. Particularly when dealing with integrated global industries, the impossibility of defining and then measuring the 'dumping' of products or the 'potential for predatory behaviour' must simply be admitted.

The burden of proof and enforcement in such cases should rest with competition policy, not with trade or FDI policy. This recommendation is a natural consequence of the neutrality principle towards foreign and domestic firms. If the actions of either create a monopolistic situation, or threaten effective competition in the home market, then antitrust actions should be initiated. However, the definition of competition in the home market should take account of foreign sources from both imports and inward FDI. In many countries – Japan is a particular example – the national apparatus for competition policy is out-of-date and inappropriate to conditions of global market players.

Again, some might argue that an international authority for competition policy is needed to guard consumer interests as global companies and their law firms shift bases to those areas affording the laxest legislative environment. The potential for monopolistic behaviour by global companies was mentioned above as a possible systemic problem brought on by FDI-led market integration. However, courts in the major consuming countries have not been reluctant to rule extraterritorially when they have felt the home market to be threatened by foreign companies' actions – even actions taken offshore. A recent example is the New York State court decision that blocked the takeover of a UK-owned mining firm, Consolidated Goldfields, by a South Africa-controlled firm which also had large gold interests. The American court ruled that the interests of US consumers could be threatened if such a large part of global gold production were to be controlled by a single firm. Since some of the assets of Consolidated Goldfields were located in the US, the New York court's decision was able to prevent the takeover.

Extraterritoriality raises difficult foreign policy issues (Rosenthal and Knighton, 1982), and is a poor substitute for a world constitution and court. In the absence of the latter, one of the major challenges of the next decade is likely to be the reconciliation of different national approaches to competition and merger policy. As part of the 1992 process the EC is strengthening its rules and centralizing its procedures in this area. But there is a very real danger that it may become so preoccupied with the problems of internal compromise among the 12 member states that it ends up with a mechanism and policy direction fundamentally at odds with that adopted in the US in the early 1980s when the basic reform of its antitrust laws took place. Canada recently tightened its reporting and notification requirements for prospective mergers. Japan has long turned a blind eye towards company activities that would be 'anti-competitive' in the US or Europe.

Just as, among major economies, FDI has become a more important linkage than trade, so competition policy has the potential to overtake trade policy as the most contentious area of international economic relations. The lack of an overall framework for competition policy runs risks in two directions.

First, there is the spectre of predatory behaviour by global companies. Although this is an important public concern, the evidence for it as a growing threat is not strong. The other – and, in many respects, opposite – risk is that national courts and regulatory authorities are becoming important obstacles to cross-border mergers and acquisitions that do *not* threaten competition. When UK-based BAT Industries tried to acquire the US insurance company Eagle Star, it had to win approval from the state insurance regulator in every state in which Eagle Star operated. It eventually succeeded, but at considerable expense and after extensive delay. It is ironic that those same insurance regulators may now prevent the takeover of BAT by another international consortium. Whether one is worried about such obstacles to international competition among global firms or about protection against the prospect of global monopolies, more uniformity is needed in antitrust provisions and enforcement across the major investing countries.

Employment creation, technology transfer and local content rules
Perhaps surprisingly, the aspect of FDI that has attracted the most policy attention in the European Community has been the attempt to increase and capture its indirect benefits in terms of employment and technology transfer. There is concern about 'screwdriver plants' which assemble products designed and produced elsewhere and there is competition among countries to attract FOFs into their slowest growing regions. How sensible are such policies? It was

noted in Chapter 3 that the employment benefits claimed for inward investment are generally overstated because many of the 'new' workers will be moving from other jobs. However, if the FDI can be attracted to an area of high unemployment then the marginal employment gain is likely to be larger.

While this argument for regional grants is valid in theory, it needs close examination in practice to make sure that the incremental benefits justify the extra costs. Since the direct benefits of FDI in the EC are likely to be much larger than its indirect benefits, the basic judgment must be whether particular policies to increase indirect benefits will at the same time reduce direct benefits, either by distorting the production choice of the FOF or by causing it to locate elsewhere.

Policies to thwart 'screwdriver plants' are likely to fail this test. By striking at the fundamental decision of an FOF regarding the global organization of its production, policies requiring a minimum level of 'local content' will have three negative side-effects. First, they run foul of the first neutrality condition by differing in their treatment of FOFs and domestic firms (which face no such requirements). This invites retaliation and builds a protectionist screen for local firms. The effect is often perverse, as domestic firms begin to source overseas while FOFs build their links to local suppliers. Consumers suffer in the short term by paying higher prices, and local producers may well suffer in the long term as the FOFs gain market knowledge and security of supply. In many respects this has been the story of the television market in the United States, although protectionism there was not due to local content requirements (Prestowitz, 1988).

Second, local content requirements distort the trade/investment decision when they are imposed in connection with a dumping complaint. Other things being equal, they will favour serving the target market through investment rather than trade. This distortion in favour of investment – which may come in the form of mergers or acquisitions – can work to the detriment of competing local firms by bidding up asset and factor prices beyond what they would have been if the trade/investment choice were a policy-neutral one.

Finally, as a practical matter, the way that local content ratios are calculated involves many arbitrary accounting and cost-assignment assumptions for which there is no economic rationale (Hindley, 1988). Thus, even if such requirements were desirable, in practice their use leads to more distortions as firms try to manage their inputs

101

and skew their accounts to avoid potential challenges on local content grounds. For all of these reasons, the EC should work to disallow, rather than harmonize, local content requirements. To the extent that they cause the FOF to change the structure of its production (which is, after all, the purpose of such policies), there will be a loss in efficiency borne both by domestic producers and by consumers.

In some cases local content targets or requirements are negotiated as a quid pro quo for investment subsidies or tax holidays. Such incentives to attract FDI to a particular location run exactly the same international risks as those which accompany export credit subsidies. If they are matched by incentives offered by competitor governments, then eventually they are bid up to the point where the foreign company captures all of the benefit that would otherwise have gone to the host economy. It is for this reason that the OECD promotes agreements to control export credit, and the European Commission reviews location incentives offered by member states. Perhaps because of such EC oversight, incentives offered to foreign investors are becoming less prevalent. The 1989 decision by Honda to build its first European plant in the UK, for example, was not associated with any special incentive although several countries were involved in the competition.

Reciprocal market access
The final case which might provide the grounds for an exception to the general policy principles for FDI is the thorny issue of reciprocal market access. There are two main areas where this arises. The first is in heavily regulated service sectors such as banking or telecommunications. Those countries which have been at the forefront of liberalization or privatization in such sectors are naturally concerned that their industries are exposed to external competition in their home markets while being unable to compete in the markets of their foreign rivals. This is a classic problem of trade policy as it moves into services.

A key item on the agenda of the Uruguay Round of GATT negotiations on services is to provide the 'right of establishment' to foreign service providers who meet non-discriminatory domestic requirements. Within the 12 countries of the EC, the 1992 objective is set even higher: to ensure freedom of movement of services throughout the Community by mutually recognizing one another's certification and qualification procedures (Nicolaides, 1989). Thus, if a bank (or a doctor) is authorized to do business in any one EC country, it (he or she) can open an office in any other without further certification. While progress along these routes is likely to come in fits and starts, such multilateral negotiations must remain the preferred vehicle for resolving issues of market access that concern different regulatory regimes.

Another group in the Uruguay Round negotiations is working specifically on trade-related investment measures (TRIMs). The United States was the key protagonist in favour of including this topic in the Round, the European Community was lukewarm, while the developing countries were initially opposed to inclusion. The US tabled its proposal in July 1989, with four elements:

(1) TRIMS which, by their nature, produce adverse trade effects should be prohibited;
(2) Other TRIMS should (a) be applied on a non-discriminatory basis and (b) be used in ways which do not produce adverse trade effects;
(3) TRIMs should be transparently reported to all;
(4) Adequate arrangements for dispute settlement should be agreed with countermeasures of 'equivalent commercial effect' allowed against countries that ignore a negative finding.

The US proposal is almost certainly too ambitious for most of the other participants. The EC has proposed that only TRIMs directed at the imports and exports of a company with the aim of influencing its trading pattern be considered. In this way it hopes to avoid challenges to its own rules on local content, which would certainly fail elements (2) and (3) of the US proposal. However, both the EC and the US have more important priorities in the Uruguay Round than a firm agreement on TRIMs. The negotiating group represents a useful initial step in this area that can be followed up in subsequent rounds, but it is unlikely to produce an agreement that has much impact on FDI flows or trade. This is an area where a tighter adherence to the OECD guidelines already signed by all of the major investing countries would bring more immediate rewards.

The second area where issues of market access arise is in takeovers and mergers. At a general level, this too is a case of differential regulations which cause firms in some countries to be more exposed to takeovers (usually by both domestic and foreign bidders) than are firms in other countries. In practice, it is much more than differential regulations regarding bids. Vulnerability to takeover derives from the structure of share-holdings, the relative use of debt and equity in different countries, the depth of the stock markets and, indeed, business ethics and cultural norms. Where differences in these factors are large, there is little prospect of narrowing them through negotiated changes in regulations by one country or the other, and there is no equivalent to 'mutual recognition' of each other's system. Frustration is bound to result. Calls for a 'level playing field' recur promptly in the UK whenever a takeover offer comes from bid-proof companies in Switzerland or Germany.

In 1989 the US and Japan set in train a process to study 'structural impediments to trade' in both their countries, while recognizing that progress is bound to be very slow. In some cases it may be possible to identify certain laws or practices which explicitly discriminate against FOFs and which can be modified or repealed. In most cases, however, the situation in the two markets is simply different – but non-discriminatory as regards domestic and foreign firms in each market. Then it must simply be admitted that a completely level playing field is an impossibility when the two teams originate from different legal, cultural, or even economic, environments. To claim that such differences make trade unfair leads to absurdities such as the proposed amendment to the 1988 US Trade Bill that would have limited imports from developing countries whose workers received 'unfairly' low wages.

In addition, there are usually two sides to the question of which 'differences' constitute unfair trade advantages. While UK companies face a higher takeover risk, it is possible to argue that they have been successful in building such large overseas assets partly because they benefited from sophisticated financial markets at home whose depth was due to a strong foreign presence. The discipline forced on US managers by the threat of takeover also may have sharpened their competitive skills and increased the responsiveness and flexibility of the US industrial structure to economic shifts. Similarly, the German system of worker participation may have conferred upon German companies an advantage of a loyal work-force, albeit with the highest wages in Europe. The supposed advantage that Japanese companies derive from their system of lifetime employment and hierarchical management may backfire as they find it hard to attract good foreign managers to run overseas subsidiaries.

In an integrated world economy, the cross-country diversity of social and economic systems is a driving force for trade and investment. There is bound to be competition between systems which, over the short term, creates profit opportunities for FOFs and stimulates FDI. Over the long term it also produces pressure for policy convergence, as we have seen. But many differences will remain. There is always a temptation to use them to justify protection. The public must be reminded that non-discriminatory differences create the rationale for the trade and investment linkages between economies that bring gains to all.

The world economy in the 1990s
We have explored the phenomenon of FDI-led integration from the perspective of the international investors – led by the United States, Britain and Japan – and that of the host economies. We have seen how it has transformed the meaning of trade flows and how the sales and purchases of foreign-owned firms in their host countries have overtaken cross-border sales (i.e., exports and imports) to become the dominant link with foreign markets. This development is likely to shift the international policy focus from trade disputes to clashes among national regulatory and competition policies. Pressures to relax these will work to open markets to investment in much the same way as tariff cuts through the successive GATT rounds stimulated trade.

Unless a major economic recession or a political backlash against inward FDI sets in, a near doubling of current levels in real terms is feasible by 1995. Global flows of around \$230 billion per year (in today's prices) result from a scenario that assumes Japan and other advanced countries begin to catch up with the international diversification that American and British firms have already achieved. Europe – East and West – becomes the focus for the greatest increase in inward flows, but this level of total investment implies that the rest of the OECD and some of the developing countries also receive major increases. If the spread of FDI in the 1990s follows the pattern of trade expansion in the 1950s, then we can expect to see a rapid and wide dispersion of flows across countries.

105

Any stimulus as large and widespread as this is bound to be a spur to economic growth. As new sectors in different countries are pulled into the stream of the global market, productivity levels will rise toward those of their world-class competitors and prices to consumers will fall. The countries of the European Community hope to reap an additional growth of 5% of their combined GNP from the 1992 process of market integration (Cecchini *et al.*, 1988). Others have suggested that when dynamic effects are taken into account, gains could be several times that figure (Baldwin, 1989). The OECD as a whole, where most of the increased FDI will go, is at a much earlier stage of integration than the EC. The impetus to growth should thus be even greater. And, as discussed in Chapter 4, greater integration of the real markets for goods and services makes the world economy more resistant to shocks, at least from the financial markets.

This rosy picture of FDI-led integration and growth is what the ivory-towered economist sees. From corporate headquarters, or in Whitehall or Washington, things look very different. Exchange rates lurch, as one news item overtakes another, and sometimes ride off in the 'wrong' direction for weeks on end before jolting back to reality. Familiar indicators like trade balances and monetary aggregates misbehave capriciously, confusing the corporate planner and provoking the government spokesman into more and more convoluted justifications of current policy. Although the G-7 heads of government continue to meet, their joint proclamations have little effect on markets because they have neither an anchor nor a consistent target for policy. In a phrase coined by Labour MP George Robertson at a 1989 Chatham House debate on British foreign policy, there is 'a bonfire of the certainties'.

Below the fog of macroeconomic policy, the new competitive pressures created by global markets are becoming painfully clear to business. Their home base is invaded by foreign entrants offering new products and service packages to their long-term, but perhaps no longer so loyal, customers. Some of their domestic competitors have joined forces with, or been acquired by, foreign rivals. New industrial structures are emerging, but without a clear trend to follow. Some companies are broadening their range of products through international acquisition and investment in related fields. At the same time, many large conglomerates are being split up and shareholders are finding that the sum of the parts is more valuable than the whole. Fewer and fewer companies, of whatever size, can consider themselves immune to the possibility of takeover.

While shareholders and consumers are the major beneficiaries of these stronger competitive forces, they too may find some of the changes difficult. Many have grown up with the familiar, if inefficient, monopolies that provide their postal service and telephone system. There are new information costs involved in choice, as US consumers discovered when they had to choose between the many alternatives to 'Ma Bell' after the removal of AT&T's monopoly over local telephone service. During the early years of airline deregulation, schedules to consumers were disrupted and delays increased – partly because of much higher demand resulting from plummeting airfares – as new airlines jostled for market position and the 'hub-spoke' system came into its own.

Is the world economy of the 1990s, driven by FDI-led market integration, likely to be a better or a worse place than the 1980s? The answer depends partly on the vantage-point and partly on the trade-off between stability and change. For those countries outside the OECD, economic growth remains the overriding priority. They should fare better in the 1990s as higher levels of growth in their export markets spur domestic production and relax foreign exchange constraints.

For many OECD countries, growth is no longer the overriding priority. Both wider concerns – the environment, drugs, the political development of Eastern Europe – and more parochial ones – the school system, reform of the health service – will often dominate macroeconomic objectives. But these other issues can be most successfully dealt with if underlying economic growth in the OECD is strong and inflation is held under control by the joint efforts of the G-7.

There are two internally generated risks that could push this scenario off the rails. The first is that economic policy-makers give undue importance to indicators such as current account balances that are increasingly unsuited to the problems of managing integrated economies. This could lead either to overly rigid attempts to stabilize exchange rates among major currencies or to unnecessary overshooting as governments try to move rates further and further to correct what they erroneously regard as dangerous imbalances.

Such mistaken macroeconomic cooperation would create an

unstable and contentious environment that could easily degenerate into economic blocs of nations with limited flows of trade and investment between them. This paper has tried to demonstrate the increasingly partial and therefore flawed nature of traditional balance-of-payments measures in a world of FDI-led market integration and floating exchange rates. But more work is clearly needed to develop and refine the new analytical concepts required and to subject the new hypotheses to rigorous test.

The second risk is a political one. Wise leadership and public education will be required to recognize the necessary link between the competitive turbulence of open markets – for both trade and investment – at the micro level and the underpinning and stimulus to growth that FDI brings at the macro level. Instability and disruption for a particular company or set of consumers will always provoke cries for protection, for the levelling of playing fields, for the exclusion of foreign competitors. As more of those competitors move in, there is a natural tendency to view it as a sudden and unique national phenomenon. The popular outcry against Japanese investment in the US is a case in point.

The antidote to this is for politicians and the public they represent to be made aware that their own situation is but a particular example of an international investment wave, a wave in which many of their own companies are a part, and a wave which will bring widespread benefits. In mature democracies, the only lasting protection against political extremism is a well-informed public. However, if leaders are preoccupied with immediate and particular concerns, there is a risk that the lessons of trade protectionism will have to be painfully relearned with FDI.

APPENDIX: FDI DATA SOURCES AND USES

BY STEPHEN THOMSEN

This appendix provides data on FDI outflows and inflows for each of the G-5 countries in real (1980 prices) and nominal terms, and in local currencies and US dollars. In the introduction to each country's data, we mention the principal government agencies collecting data on FDI in each country and give a definition of FDI adopted by each country. In spite of the work at the IMF and the OECD on harmonizing definitions of FDI, there are still important differences across countries and, as a result, divergences in recorded bilateral flows. For this reason, FDI figures should be interpreted cautiously, and direct comparison should be made with the FOF measures provided in this paper and with other countries' statistics.

The United States
The US data on FDI come from the Bureau of Economic Analysis in the Department of Commerce and are published annually in the August issues of the *Survey of Current Business* (*SCB*). They are revised on the basis of periodic Benchmark Surveys of both inward and outward FDI which appear every five years or so. The latest survey of inward investment is based on 1987 data and has just been published. For outward FDI, the latest survey is still based on 1982 data, published in 1985. In addition to the Benchmark Surveys, the Bureau of Economic Analysis conducts annual surveys based on a smaller sample of firms. These nevertheless include a large share of the total FDI. The two data sets provide a comprehensive set of information on the activities of US MNEs abroad and of FOFs in the US, relating not just to balance-of-payments measures of FDI flows but also figures on sales, employment, exports, imports, etc.

109

The US follows the OECD guidelines on classification of FDIs, requiring a minimum foreign ownership of 10% of the voting stock of an enterprise and including retained earnings. The data in Table A.1 have been adjusted for finance affiliates of US MNEs located in the Netherlands Antilles. These affiliates were generally established by US MNEs to raise capital in the Euromarket without paying the 30% US withholding tax on interest payments to foreigners because of a special tax treaty between the US and that country. Although the US has similar tax treaties with other countries, US MNEs preferred the Netherlands Antilles because it does not have a withholding tax of its own and because it structures most taxes on affiliates to generate offsetting tax credits for US parent firms (*SCB*, August 1983, p. 15).

The US withholding tax was repealed in July 1984 and as a result the finance affiliates are no longer necessary. Consequently, the US investment position in the Netherlands Antilles has declined in every year since 1984. The use of these finance affiliates meant that the US outward FDI position was understated by as much as $25 billion in 1984, falling to roughly $11 billion by 1988. Until the repeal of the US withholding tax in 1984, FDI outflows were understated by the amount of borrowing of US MNEs from their affiliates in the Netherlands Antilles. Since 1985, however, borrowing has virtually ceased while repayments of previous borrowing have increased substantially. Annual outflows of US FDI are now overstated by only about $3 billion as a result of including these affiliates.

Because these affiliates were created for the purpose of avoiding the US withholding tax when borrowing in the Euromarket, the capital which flows between the finance affiliate and the parent, though recorded as FDI, is actually related to international borrowing. We have therefore eliminated the Netherlands Antilles from the aggregate FDI data. Figure A.1 shows the effect of this adjustment.

Another adjustment which could be made to the US data (but which was not for the purposes of this study) would be to remove the direct effect of exchange rate gains and losses on the earnings of the foreign affiliates. Under US accounting laws (FASB 52), foreign-currency-denominated assets and liabilities are translated into dollars at the current or average exchange rate. An exception is made for countries with very high rates of inflation. All capital gains and losses resulting from translation are included in the income statement of the affiliates. This affects the FDI figures through its impact on retained earnings. An appreciation of the dollar leads to a capital loss when translating foreign assets into dollars. This lowers the income of the affiliates and hence decreases recorded US FDI outflows. The US accounting rule FASB 52 dates from December 1982. Prior to that, historical rather than current exchange rates were used to translate certain items, so the effect on the data was less (*SCB*, August 1984, p. 22).

Figure A.1   US outflows of FDI, adjusted and unadjusted (US $ bn)

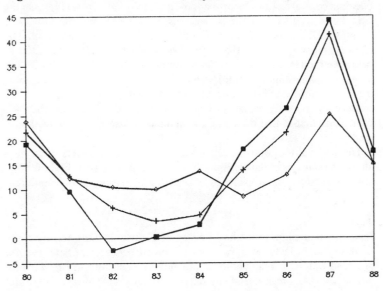

I. Unadjusted US FDI outflows.
II. Adjusted for the Netherlands Antilles.
III. Adjusted for the Netherlands Antilles and exchange rate gains and losses.

Translation gains and losses are purely an accounting concept and should not be confused with exchange rate movements which might affect the competitiveness and hence the profitability of the affiliate. The reason why this study did not remove translation gains and losses from the US data is that the other countries in the sample do not provide comparable figures to enable a similar adjustment to be made to their data. To minimize the distorting effect of exchange rate movements over the period, all cross-country comparisons are based on growth rates calculated in each country's local currency.

Figure A1 provides an idea of how the adjustments affect recorded FDI flows. The two adjustments serve to dampen the apparent volatility of FDI flows. The unadjusted flows record net disinvestment by US MNEs in 1982, leading some to conclude at the time that US MNEs were returning home to benefit from the US economic miracle. In fact, if both adjustments are made, the US recorded an outflow of $10.5 billion.

The United Kingdom

UK data come from the Department of Trade and Industry (DTI). Like the US, the UK adheres to the suggestions of the IMF and the OECD in defining FDI, except that there is a 20% minimum ownership level. The parent company's share in the retained earnings of the affiliate is included. Although the UK has a similar definition of FDI to the US (except for the minimum ownership threshold), there is a discrepancy between the data of the two countries. This is due in part to different accounting practices concerning company stocks and work-in-progress. In the UK they are valued on a first-in-first-out basis, and in the US a last-in-first-out method is used.

The book value of outward and inward FDI is provided every three years although estimates of the aggregate levels are made each year. FDI outflows of UK oil companies are excluded before 1975 for reasons of confidentiality.

Japan

Japanese data come from the Ministry of Finance (MOF) and from the Bank of Japan. Data from the latter are on a calendar year basis and are provided only for total outflows and inflows. The Ministry of Finance provides a disaggregation of the data, by fiscal year. However, the total figures from the Ministry are considerably higher than those from the Bank of Japan. This is because the latter are recorded according to standard balance-of-payments accounting practices, while the former are based on approvals of FDI by the MOF before 1980 and on notifications thereafter. This study uses the Bank of Japan data because they are recorded in a manner consistent with the methodology of other countries.

In a comparison with foreign data sources, Japanese figures from the Ministry of Finance are much higher than the inflows of Japanese FDI reported by other countries. FDI inflows to Japan, on the other hand, are understated relative to what other countries record as their outward FDI to Japan from their firms. An upward bias in the Ministry of Finance statistics may result from the fact that Japanese companies overstate the scope of their prospective investments abroad so as not to have to file again with the Ministry should their plans expand. This possibility was obviously much more likely when outward FDI required approval by the Ministry.

Japanese data exclude retained earnings. Prior to 1980, Japanese data on outward FDI were based on a 25% minimum stock ownership. The current minimum is 10% for outflows. There is no acknowledged minimum for inflows. Table A.4 provides FDI figures from the Bank of Japan. Because the Japanese government records much of its data in US dollars in its English-language sources, the figures have been reconverted back into yen using the period average exchange rate.

Appendix: FDI data sources and uses

Germany

All German data come from the Bundesbank. They include retained earnings and are based on a 25% minimum ownership. Figures for the total stock of FDI are available only since 1976.

France

The French data come from the Banque de France and the Ministère de l'Economie et des Finances. Like the UK, France uses a 20% ownership rule although any investment may be considered FDI if it can be established that the investor has effective control over the other firm with less than 20% of the voting stock. Figures for the stock of FDI are not provided and retained earnings are not included.

Table A.1 FDI from and to the United States
(millions of current and constant-1980 dollars)

	Outflows		Inflows	
	Current	Constant	Current	Constant
1961	2,653	7,288	311	854
1962	2,852	7,646	346	928
1963	3,483	9,214	231	611
1964	3,759	9,789	322	839
1965	5,010	12,716	415	1,053
1966	5,416	13,275	425	1,042
1967	4,807	11,473	698	1,666
1968	5,295	12,034	807	1,834
1969	5,960	12,845	1,263	2,722
1970	7,590	15,490	1,464	2,988
1971	7,618	14,707	367	708
1972	7,747	14,293	949	1,751
1973	11,435	19,784	2,800	4,844
1974	9,052	14,368	4,760	7,556
1975	14,244	20,584	2,603	3,762
1976	11,949	16,235	4,347	5,906
1977	14,254	18,158	3,728	4,749
1978	16,911	20,060	7,897	9,368
1979	26,993	29,436	11,877	12,952
1980	22,750	22,750	16,918	16,918
1981	14,509	13,238	25,195	22,988
1982	16,277	13,948	13,792	11,818
1983	5,815	4,798	11,946	9,856
1984	6,676	5,303	25,359	20,142
1985	13,860	10,621	19,022	14,576
1986	21,445	16,112	34,091	25,613
1987	41,202	30,053	46,894	34,204
1988	14,805	10,383	58,436	40,984

Table A.2 FDI from and to the United Kingdom
(millions of current and constant-1980 pounds)

	Outflows		Inflows	
	Current	Constant	Current	Constant
1961	226	1,222	236	1,276
1962	209	1,088	130	677
1963	236	1,204	160	816
1964	263	1,296	162	798
1965	308	1,446	197	925
1966	276	1,238	196	879
1967	281	1,222	170	739
1968	410	1,715	274	1,146
1969	549	2,179	322	1,278
1970	546	2,014	363	1,339
1971	676	2,283	450	1,520
1972	737	2,296	408	1,271
1973	1,621	4,712	734	2,134
1974	1,576	3,990	854	2,162
1975	1,324	2,632	1,518	3,018
1976	2,419	4,200	1,653	2,870
1977	2,399	3,657	2,546	3,881
1978	3,520	4,829	1,962	2,691
1979	5,889	7,053	3,030	3,629
1980	4,886	4,886	4,355	4,355
1981	6,093	5,465	2,932	2,630
1982	4,091	3,406	3,027	2,520
1983	5,417	4,292	3,386	2,683
1984	6,033	4,591	(181)	(138)
1985	8,799	6,263	3,784	2,693
1986	11,304	7,716	4,846	3,308
1987	18,615	12,159	8,108	5,296
1988	15,219	9,476	7,346	4,574

Table A.3 FDI from and to the United Kingdom
(millions of current and constant-1980 dollars)

	Outflows		Inflows	
	Current	Constant	Current	Constant
1961	633	3,423	661	3,575
1962	587	3,056	365	1,901
1963	661	3,372	448	2,286
1964	734	3,618	452	2,228
1965	861	4,043	551	2,586
1966	771	3,457	547	2,455
1967	772	3,356	467	2,030
1968	981	4,106	656	2,744
1969	1,312	5,208	770	3,054
1970	1,308	4,827	870	3,209
1971	1,652	5,581	1,100	3,716
1972	1,844	5,745	1,021	3,180
1973	3,975	11,555	1,800	5,232
1974	3,686	9,332	1,998	5,057
1975	2,906	5,777	3,373	6,705
1976	4,261	7,398	2,986	5,183
1977	4,095	6,242	4,444	6,774
1978	6,778	9,298	3,766	5,166
1979	12,503	14,974	6,428	7,699
1980	11,531	11,531	10,131	10,131
1981	12,536	11,243	5,946	5,333
1982	7,193	5,989	5,299	4,412
1983	8,195	6,494	5,137	4,070
1984	8,141	6,196	(242)	(184)
1985	11,406	8,118	4,905	3,491
1986	16,583	11,319	7,109	4,853
1987	30,508	19,927	13,288	8,679
1988	27,111	16,881	13,086	8,148

Table A.4 FDI from and to Japan
(millions of current and constant-1980 yen)

	Outflows		Inflows	
	Current	Constant	Current	Constant
1961	33,587	98,785	15,891	46,737
1962	27,783	78,929	16,237	46,128
1963	44,101	119,838	32,172	87,423
1964	20,632	53,730	30,405	79,181
1965	27,835	76,828	16,990	46,895
1966	38,771	102,030	10,871	28,607
1967	44,544	110,259	16,297	40,338
1968	79,321	186,638	27,402	64,475
1969	73,824	165,525	25,803	57,853
1970	127,115	264,823	33,659	70,122
1971	124,882	246,315	73,051	144,084
1972	218,889	408,375	51,236	95,589
1973	517,045	854,620	(11,411)	(18,862)
1974	845,864	1,157,132	59,000	80,712
1975	522,944	664,478	67,075	85,228
1976	590,135	700,041	33,510	39,751
1977	441,967	495,479	5,639	6,321
1978	498,953	533,640	1,684	1,801
1979	635,068	659,468	52,374	54,387
1980	541,002	541,002	63,034	63,034
1981	1,079,984	1,046,496	41,682	40,390
1982	1,131,072	1,076,187	109,346	104,040
1983	857,886	810,091	98,804	93,299
1984	1,417,044	1,321,870	(2,375)	(2,216)
1985	1,542,161	1,416,126	153,143	140,627
1986	2,440,001	2,194,246	38,086	34,250
1987	2,823,228	2,550,342	168,506	152,218
1988	4,374,785	3,924,457	(62,665)	(56,215)

Table A.5 FDI from and to Japan
(millions of current and constant-1980 dollars)

	Outflows		Inflows	
	Current	Constant	Current	Constant
1961	93	274	44	129
1962	77	219	45	128
1963	122	332	89	242
1964	57	148	84	219
1965	77	213	47	130
1966	107	282	30	79
1967	123	304	45	111
1968	220	518	76	179
1969	206	462	72	161
1970	355	740	94	196
1971	359	708	210	414
1972	722	1,347	169	315
1973	1,903	3,145	(42)	(69)
1974	2,896	3,962	202	276
1975	1,762	2,239	226	287
1976	1,990	2,361	113	134
1977	1,646	1,845	21	24
1978	2,371	2,536	8	9
1979	2,898	3,009	239	248
1980	2,386	2,386	278	278
1981	4,897	4,745	189	183
1982	4,541	4,321	439	418
1983	3,612	3,411	416	393
1984	5,966	5,565	(10)	(9)
1985	6,465	5,937	642	590
1986	14,479	13,021	226	203
1987	19,519	17,632	1,165	1,052
1988	34,138	30,624	(489)	(439)

Table A.6 FDI from and to Germany
(millions of current and constant-1980 DM)

	Outflows		Inflows	
	Current	Constant	Current	Constant
1961	820	1,889	1,332	3,069
1962	1,139	2,526	1,444	3,202
1963	865	1,860	2,010	4,323
1964	1,192	2,489	2,532	5,286
1965	1,242	2,499	3,660	7,364
1966	1,427	2,783	4,061	7,916
1967	1,343	2,583	3,361	6,463
1968	1,980	3,729	2,163	4,073
1969	2,787	5,031	2,067	3,731
1970	3,194	5,360	2,176	3,651
1971	3,656	5,677	3,905	6,064
1972	4,990	7,360	6,157	9,081
1973	4,418	6,127	5,324	7,384
1974	4,958	6,423	5,495	7,118
1975	4,940	6,039	1,690	2,066
1976	6,179	7,287	3,378	3,983
1977	5,123	5,821	2,249	2,556
1978	7,241	7,896	3,270	3,566
1979	8,235	8,632	3,194	3,348
1980	7,596	7,596	771	771
1981	8,727	8,391	770	740
1982	6,020	5,543	1,988	1,831
1983	8,094	7,220	4,533	4,044
1984	12,492	10,929	1,573	1,376
1985	14,142	12,108	1,727	1,479
1986	20,874	17,337	2,357	1,958
1987	16,242	13,216	3,472	2,825
1988	18,250	14,673	2,851	2,292

Table A.7 FDI from and to Germany
(millions of current and constant-1980 dollars)

	Outflows		Inflows	
	Current	Constant	Current	Constant
1961	204	470	331	764
1962	285	632	361	801
1963	217	467	504	1,084
1964	300	626	637	1,330
1965	311	626	916	1,844
1966	357	696	1,016	1,980
1967	337	648	843	1,621
1968	496	934	542	1,020
1969	710	1,282	527	951
1970	876	1,470	597	1,001
1971	1,050	1,630	1,121	1,741
1972	1,565	2,308	1,931	2,848
1973	1,653	2,293	1,992	2,763
1974	1,916	2,482	2,123	2,751
1975	2,008	2,455	687	840
1976	2,454	2,894	1,342	1,582
1977	2,206	2,507	968	1,101
1978	3,605	3,931	1,628	1,775
1979	4,493	4,710	1,743	1,827
1980	4,179	4,179	424	424
1981	4,096	3,938	341	328
1982	2,782	2,562	819	754
1983	3,170	2,828	1,775	1,584
1984	4,401	3,850	553	484
1985	4,803	4,112	587	502
1986	9,613	7,984	1,085	902
1987	9,036	7,353	1,932	1,572
1988	10,392	8,355	1,623	1,305

Table A.8 FDI from and to France
(millions of current and constant-1980 francs)

	Outflows		Inflows	
	Current	Constant	Current	Constant
1961	1,702	6,235	863	3,162
1962	1,455	5,089	1,230	4,301
1963	902	2,966	1,039	3,417
1964	965	3,045	1,137	3,586
1965	1,294	3,994	1,162	3,585
1966	1,135	3,409	1,238	3,718
1967	1,619	4,705	1,569	4,562
1968	1,693	4,717	981	2,733
1969	395	1,034	1,599	4,186
1970	2,062	5,104	3,461	8,567
1971	2,188	5,125	2,910	6,815
1972	3,005	6,633	3,467	7,653
1973	4,168	8,524	5,011	10,247
1974	3,765	6,933	8,882	16,357
1975	6,108	9,915	6,247	10,141
1976	8,184	12,107	5,022	7,429
1977	5,885	7,953	8,670	11,716
1978	8,095	9,933	11,031	13,535
1979	8,395	9,349	11,579	12,894
1980	13,260	13,260	14,061	14,061
1981	25,079	22,513	13,184	11,835
1982	20,133	16,184	10,275	8,260
1983	14,029	10,270	12,433	9,102
1984	18,580	12,665	19,212	13,096
1985	20,000	12,887	19,858	12,795
1986	36,227	22,266	19,039	11,702
1987	52,302	31,242	27,766	16,586
1988	75,972	44,188	42,909	24,957

Table A.9 FDI from and to France
(millions of current and constant-1980 dollars)

| | Outflows | | Inflows | |
	Current	Constant	Current	Constant
1961	347	1,271	176	645
1962	297	1,038	251	878
1963	184	605	212	697
1964	197	621	232	732
1965	264	815	237	731
1966	231	694	252	757
1967	329	956	319	927
1968	342	953	196	552
1969	76	199	307	805
1970	373	923	626	1,550
1971	397	930	528	1,236
1972	595	1,313	687	1,516
1973	935	1,912	1,124	2,299
1974	782	1,440	1,845	3,398
1975	1,425	2,313	1,457	2,366
1976	1,712	2,533	1,051	1,555
1977	1,197	1,618	1,764	2,384
1978	1,891	2,320	2,444	2,999
1979	1,983	2,208	2,722	3,031
1980	3,100	3,100	3,328	3,328
1981	4,583	4,114	2,426	2,178
1982	2,844	2,286	1,563	1,257
1983	1,700	1,245	1,631	1,194
1984	2,134	1,455	2,198	1,499
1985	2,226	1,434	2,210	1,424
1986	5,231	3,215	2,749	1,690
1987	8,701	5,198	4,619	2,759
1988	12,754	7,418	7,203	4,190

REFERENCES

Alexander, Sidney S. (1952). *Effects of a Devaluation on a Trade Balance*, IMF Staff Papers, April.

Baldwin, Richard (1989). 'The Growth Effects of 1992', *Economic Policy*, No. 9, November.

Batra, R.N., and R. Ramachandran (1980). 'Multinational Firms, and the Theory of International Trade and Investment', *American Economic Review*, No. 70.

Bergsten, C. Fred (1988). 'The Case for Target Zones', in C. Fred Bergsten *et al.*, *The International Monetary System: The Next Twenty-Five Years*, Washington, DC, Per Jacobsson Foundation, International Monetary Fund.

Bhagwati, Jagdish N. (1987). *The Theory of Political Economy, Economic Policy and Foreign Investment*, Columbia University Discussion Paper Series No. 386, December.

Boltho, Andrea, and Christopher Allsopp (1987). 'The Assessment: Trade and Trade Policy', *Oxford Review of Economic Policy*, Vol. 3, No. 1, Spring.

Brech, Michael, and Margaret Sharp (1984). *Inward Investment: Policy Options for the United Kingdom*, London, Routledge/Royal Institute of International Affairs.

Buckley, P.J., and Mark Casson (1976). *The Future of the Multinational Enterprise*, London, Macmillan.

Cantwell, John (1989). *Technological Innovation and Multinational Corporations*, Oxford, Basil Blackwell.

Cecchini, P., M. Catinat and A. Jacquemin (1988). *The European Challenge: 1992; The Benefits of a Single Market*, Aldershot, Wildwood House.

References

Davenport, Michael (1989). *The Charybdis of Anti-Dumping: A New Form of EC Industrial Policy?* RIIA Discussion Papers, No. 22.

Deardorff, Alan (1985). 'Comparative Advantage and International Trade and Investment in Services', *Discussion Paper No. 5 of the Fisherman-Davidson Center for the Study of the Service Sector*, University of Pennsylvania.

Dell, Edmund (1987). *The Politics of Economic Interdependence*, London, Macmillan Press.

Dornbusch, Rudiger (1973). 'Devaluation, Money and Non-traded Goods', *American Economic Review*, December.

Dunning, John H. (1958). *American Investment in British Manufacturing Industry*, London, Allen and Unwin.

Dunning, John H. (1977). 'Trade, Location of Economic Activity and the Multinational Enterprise: A Search for an Eclectic Approach', in P.O. Hesselborn and P.M. Wijkman, eds., *The International Allocation of Economic Activity*, London, Macmillan.

Dunning, John H. (1985). *Japanese Participation in British Industry*, Beckenham, Croom Helm.

Dunning, John H. (1989). *The Study of International Business: A Plea for a More Interdisciplinary Approach*, University of Reading Discussion Paper in International Investment and Business Studies No. 127.

Frenkel, Jacob A., and Assat Razin (1987). *The Mundell-Fleming Model a Quarter Century Later*, IMF Staff Papers, December.

Frowen, Stephen, ed. (1990). *Monetary Theory and Monetary Policy: New Tracks for the 1990s*, London, Macmillan.

Graham, Edward M., and Paul Krugman (1989). *Foreign Direct Investment in the United States*, Washington, DC, Institute for International Economics.

Group of Thirty (1984). *Foreign Direct Investment, 1973–87*, New York, Group of Thirty.

Harvey-Jones, John (1988). *Making It Happen: Reflections on Leadership*, Glasgow, William Collins.

Helpman, Elhanan (1984). 'A Simple Theory of International Trade with Multinational Corporations', *Journal of Political Economy*, No. 93.

Helpman, Elhanan (1985). 'Multinational Corporations and Trade Structure', *Review of Economic Studies*, No. 52.

Henderson, David (1986). *Innocence and Design: The Influence of Economic Ideas on Policy*, Oxford, Basil Blackwell.

Henderson, David (1989). 'A New Age of Reform', *Fiscal Studies*, August.

Hindley, Brian (1988). 'Dumping and the Far East Trade of the European Community', *The World Economy*, 11(4), December.

Horst, T.O. (1971). 'The Theory of the Multinational Firm: Optimal

Behaviour under Different Tariff and Tax Rates', *Journal of Political Economy*, No. 79.

Industrial Structure Council (1986). *Outlook for Japan's Industrial Society towards the 21st Century*, Tokyo, partial translation.

Institute for International Economics [IIE] (1987). *Resolving the Global Economic Crisis: After Wall Street*, Washington, DC, Institute for International Economics.

International Monetary Fund (1977). *Balance of Payments Manual*, 4th edition, Washington, DC.

Isard, Peter (1988). 'Exchange-Rate Modelling: An Assessment of Alternative Approaches', in Ralph C. Bryant, Dale W. Henderson, Gerald Holtham, Peter Hooper and Steven A. Symansky, eds., *Empirical Macroeconomics for Interdependent Economies*, Washington, DC, Brookings.

Julius, DeAnne (1987). 'Britain's Changing International Interests: Economic Influences on Foreign Policy Priorities', *International Affairs*, Summer.

Julius, DeAnne, and Stephen E. Thomsen (1988). *Inward Investment and Foreign-owned Firms in the G-5*, RIIA Discussion Papers, No. 12.

Kenen, Peter B. (1988). *Managing Exchange Rates*, London, Routledge/ Royal Institute of International Affairs.

Kindleberger, C.P. (1969). *American Business Abroad*, New Haven, CT, Yale University Press.

Krugman, Paul (1988). 'An Imperfectly Integrated World', Robbins Memorial Lecture, London School of Economics, mimeo.

Krugman, Paul, and Maurice Obstfeld (1988). *International Economics: Theory and Policy*, Cambridge, MA, MIT Press.

McManus, J.C. (1972). 'The Theory of the International Firm', in G. Paquet, ed., *The Multinational Firm and the Nation State*, Toronto, Collier Macmillan.

Markusen, James (1984). 'Multinational, Multi-Plant Economies, and the Grains from Trade', *Journal of International Economics*, No. 16.

Marris, Stephen (1985). *Deficits and the Dollar: The World Economy at Risk*, Washington, DC, Institute for International Economics.

Meade, James (1951). *The Theory of International Economic Policy, Vol. 1: The Balance of Payments*, London, Oxford University Press.

Nicolaides, Phedon (1989). *Liberalizing Service Trade: Strategies for Success*, London, Routledge/Royal Institute of International Affairs.

OECD (1985). *Structural Adjustment and Multinational Enterprises*, Paris, OECD.

Ohmae, Kenichi (1985). *Triad Power: The Coming Shape of Global Competition*, New York, Macmillan, Inc.

References

Oliver, Nick, and Barry Wilkinson (1988). *The Japanization of British Industry*, Oxford, Basil Blackwell.

Phillips and Drew (1988). *Pension Fund Indicators: A Longterm Perspective on Pension Fund Investment*, Phillips and Drew Fund Management, London, September.

Polak, J.J. (1957). *Monetary Analysis of Income Formation*, IMF Staff Papers, November.

Prestowitz, Clyde B. Jr. (1988). *Trading Places: How We Allowed Japan to Take the Lead*, New York, Basic Books.

Riedel, Jürgen, Veronika Büttner and Angelika Ernst (1988). 'External Debt Alleviation through Foreign Direct Investment: A Real Issue for Third World Countries?', *Tokyo Club Papers*, No. 1, pp. 67–134, Tokyo.

Robinson, Joan (1937). 'The Foreign Exchanges', in her *Essays in the Theory of Employment*, Oxford, Basil Blackwell.

Rosenthal, Douglas E., and William M. Knighton (1982). *National Laws and International Commerce: The Problem of Extraterritoriality*, London, Routledge/Royal Institute of International Affairs.

Servan-Schreiber, Jean-Jacques (1968). *The American Challenge*, trans. by Ronald Steel, New York, Atheneum.

Steckler, Louis E., and William L. Helkie (1989). *Implications for Future US Net Investment Payments of Growing US Net International Indebtedness*, International Finance Discussion Papers, No. 358, Washington, DC, Board of Governors of the Federal Reserve System.

Survey of Current Business [SCB], August 1983 and August 1984.

Thomsen, Stephen E. (1988). *The Growth of American, British and Japanese Direct Investment in the 1980s*, RIIA Discussion Papers, No. 2.

Thomsen, Stephen E. (forthcoming, 1990). *Multinational Enterprise and World Trade*, Geneva, Graduate Institute of International Studies.

Tolchin, Martin, and Susan Tolchin (1987). *Buying into America*, New York, Times Books.

Tugendhat, Christopher (1971). *The Multinationals*, London, Eyre & Spottiswoode.

Turner, Louis (1987). *Industrial Collaboration with Japan*, London, Routledge/Royal Institute of International Affairs.

Vernon, Raymond (1977). *Storm over the Multinationals: The Real Issues*, London, Macmillan.

von Pfeil, Enzio (1985). *German Direct Investments in the United States*, London, JAI Press.

Woolcock, Stephen (1989). *European Mergers: European or Community Controls?*, RIIA Discussion Papers, No. 15.

Yoshitomi, Masaru (1989). *Japan's Savings and External Surplus in the World Economy*, New York and London, Group of Thirty.

The Council on Foreign Relations publishes authoritative and timely books on international affairs and American foreign policy. Designed for the interested citizen and specialist alike, the Council's rich assortment of studies covers topics ranging from economics to regional conflict to U.S.–Soviet relations. If you would like more information, please write:

Council on Foreign Relations Press
58 East 68th Street
New York, NY 10021
Telephone: (212) 734-0400
FAX: (212) 861-1789

PAID